C000120954

YOU'RE INVITED!

**Invitation Design
for Every Occasion**

gestalten

April 27, 1946
Naxos, Greece
Invitation to follow

er 23, 1905
Florence
om to follow

Save the date
to celebrate the wedding of

LUCINDA
LEPLASTRIER

and OSCAR
HOPKINS

May 7, 1888
Sydney

Invitation to follow

Save the date
to celebrate the wedding of

MARIA

Save the date
to celebrate the wedding of

GILBERTE
SWANN
and
ROBERT
DE SAINT-LOUP

July 10, 1913 | Paris
Invitation to follow

Save the date
to cel

Tactile Pleasures

Modern invitations tell a story about the event and its hosts rather than simply conveying a time and a place. As a social tool, today's invitations have evolved into something much more colorful and personal than their predecessors, which were constrained both by rigid expectations of what an invitation needed to look like and by printing limitations of the time. Traditionally, the invitation was a formal tool with the simple task of informing invitees of an event, often reproducing the language, layout, and typefaces seen elsewhere. Today, an invitation arriving in the mailbox—or inbox—is often one of a kind in terms of its design and wording, each carefully chosen to reflect the personality of its sender.

The experience of opening an invitation that arrives in the mail is just as important as attending the event itself; the moment the invitation is taken from its envelope is the moment the event begins. Upon feeling the texture of the paper and discovering the story told within its design, the recipient physically connects with the sender and touches a small piece of the day to come. As physical objects, invitations often have an afterlife and turn into cherished keepsakes or wall art.

No matter what the occasion, the modern invitation serves as a kind of *amuse-bouche* to an event. It relies on materials, illustration, typography, and color to tell the story of what's to come, and builds excitement for the day. Designer Lize-Marie Dreyer of Aurora Creative Studio (pp. 52–59) compares the most successful invitations to good movie trailers; both quickly tell a story in a compelling way that whets the recipient's appetite for more.

It is no wonder that the invitation has transformed into a tool for storytelling and branding. Most people are now familiar with the idea of telling a visual story about the personal and professional moments in their lives—why not also do so for special events? Advancements in technology and digital printing have also facilitated the trend. In addition to the traditional printing techniques of the past, designers can now print with endless colors, or deliver an invitation instantly to hundreds of inboxes. New finishing techniques such as laser cutting also enable

"A successful invitation of today will break the rules a bit."

JAMES HIRSCHFELD

also enable designers to offer their clients a range of previously unimaginable choices that cater to individual tastes and styles.

The shifts in invitation culture happened relatively quickly. While digital printing and online invitations needed time to become fully accepted means of formal invitation, they are now commonplace and here to stay— and their flexibility comes hand in hand with the current interest in customization. But just as it seemed that the paper invitation might be taking a back seat to its digital counterparts, all things tactile and handmade came back into favor. However, instead of nostalgically returning to the traditionally printed invitation of yesteryear, contemporary paper invitation culture has experienced a modern twist. Formal, predictable elements are few and far between; now the old is being mixed with the new for some exciting results.

Wedding invitations are at the forefront of invitation trends. The days of hyper-coordinated weddings are a thing of the past; couples now crave an event that is unique and reflects their personal style. When designer Lisa Hedge of Venamour (pp. 80–85) noticed the trend coming, she also saw a niche for her own style. Her invitations, with their unique mix of editorial design and luxury branding, were extremely unusual in the world of wedding stationery, but their artful and sophisticated look struck a chord with her clients. Ultimately, Hedge built a stationery business—one that provides a semi-custom experience for her clients—on the lessons she learned from observing vintage invitation design and modern sensibilities.

Despite the options that digital printing now provides, letterpress printing serves as an example of how traditional techniques can be mixed with modern technology to create contemporary invitations. Instead of using wood and metal type, Studio on Fire (pp. 162–167) uses a process that turns digital files into letterpress-friendly plates. Next, they lead clients through the options of paper, palettes, and finishing techniques to create one-of-a-kind invitations that won't be immediately—or ever—tossed in the trash. It is these extra finishing techniques that help define the modern invitation: foil stamping, calligraphy, and hand lettering, laser cutting, silk screening, and unusual folding techniques all present even

more options for branding an event and setting it apart. German studio Paperlux (pp. 22–29) is the master of this discipline: the self-described "material fetishists" create invitations of various tangible forms and textures.

A successful invitation of today will break the rules a bit, says James Hirschfeld. His company Paperless Post (pp. 210–221) was at the forefront of the digital invitation movement at a time when sending anything other than a physical event invite was unheard of. Breaking the rules can simply mean changing the form of an invitation by exchanging a piece of paper for a physical object. In the corporate world, where invitation recipients may not have a personal connection to an event or its hosts, paper invitations have a good chance of getting lost on the desks of busy journalists and PR professionals. Designers are opting instead for three-dimensional invitations—whether useful, playful, or simply too unusual to blend into the background. Often these objects are interactive—like a simple pinhole camera that not only invites the recipient to a photography show, but asks them to use the invitation to take a photo that will then form part of the exhibit. Another example is a potted basil plant—both an invitation and a culinary gift.

With so many options, creativity and logistics are part of staging an event. Designers need to address which materials and finishing techniques will accurately convey the concept of the invitation—without going overboard— as well as having to consider which elements each package needs. These include items such as save the dates, thank you cards, RSVPs, and maps. For every element there are financial considerations to keep in mind not only in terms of printing costs but also regarding envelope shape and size and mailing.

You're Invited! pays tribute to the subtle power of the well-crafted invitation as it explores the countless design, paper, and printing options available to those planning an event. Unlike brand identities or ad campaigns, invitations are a more intimate form of visual communication because they are physical objects delivered directly to a select audience. The work showcased in this book provides a glimpse into the craft of this unique form of communication and reveals the secrets of designers, wedding planners, and paper artists.❮

ALISON and **CHRIS**
are getting married
NOVEMBER 14, 2009
in **PENINSULA, OHIO**
invitation to follow

A Labor of Love

Claudia Wiesinger of BOOKS, INK. genuinely gets to know her coupled-up clients in order to perfectly personalize each wedding invitation design.

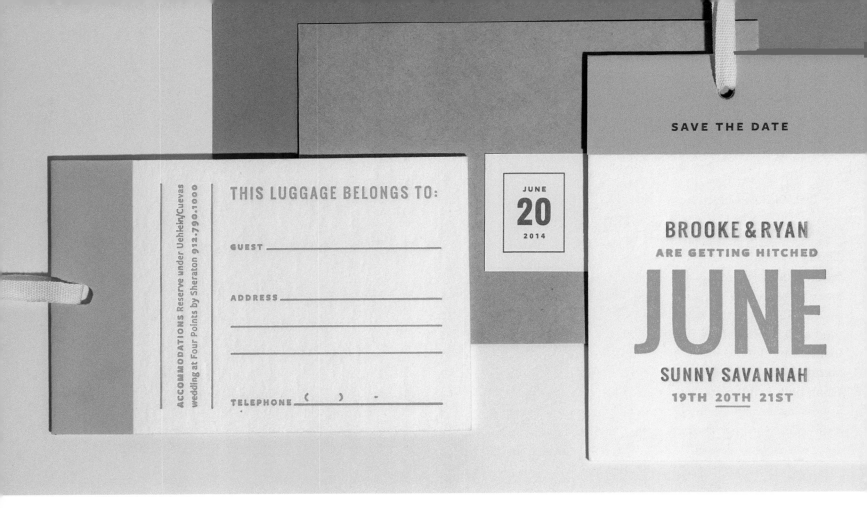

THIS LUGGAGE BELONGS TO:

GUEST

ADDRESS

TELEPHONE (   )   -

ACCOMMODATIONS Reserve under Uehlein/Cuevas wedding at Four Points by Sheraton 912·790·1000

JUNE
20
2014

BROOKE & RYAN
ARE GETTING HITCHED
JUNE
SUNNY SAVANNAH
19TH 20TH 21ST

RSVP
BY APRIL 25TH

M

06.19 • THE WELCOME DINNER
The Lady & Sons

06.20 • OUR WEDDING CELEBRATION
Orleans Square & Vic's on the River

06.21 • NEWLYWED PUB CRAWL
Downtown Savannah

SADLY REGRETS

to rsvp : detach & return in enclosed envelope

join us for a
WELCOME DINNER
THE LADY & SONS

see you in savannah

102 W CONGRESS STREET
5 O'CLOCK
coastal casual attire

Low Country Wedding

Invitations designed by
CHRISTINE WISNIESKI give guests a taste of the
Southern flair that awaits them.

Though hailing from the Midwestern United States, Brooke and Ryan decided to get married in Savannah, Georgia, and they knew it would be a colorful family affair—especially in the South. Together with designer Christine Wisnieski, they created an invitation suite that sent guests a variety of materials inspired by the low country as a lead up to their big day. The color palette combines a super saturated blue and red with blush pink and the soft brown of kraft paper. Polygon shapes appear again and again in linear patterns and die-cut forms. Letterpress printed on luxurious Italian cotton paper, the final suite is fresh and elegant—a lovely representation of the day. ‹

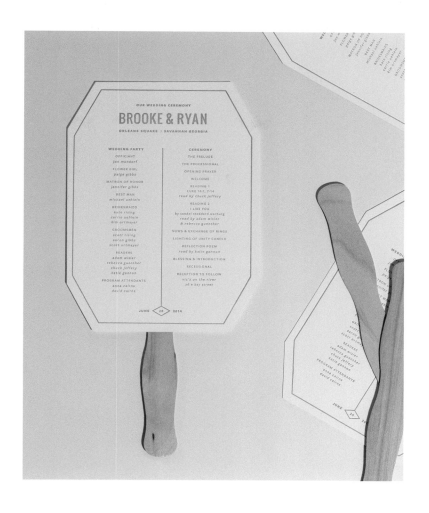

Eclectic Geometry

This colorful wedding suite designed by BLAZAR includes invitations, map, info, ceremony programme, and thank you cards and was printed with a risograph by Hato Press in London.

KELLY & STEFAN

♥

Wij gaan trouwen en nodigen u en uw partner
graag uit om erbij te zijn.

ZATERDAG
11.06.2016
· SAVE THE DATE ·

◯◯
10u30
VREDEGERECHT BORGERHOUT

Turnhoutsebaan 92, 2140 Antwerpen
Om voldoende plaats te voorzien, vragen wij u
te bevestigen of u naar de wettelijke trouw komt.

〜〜〜〜〜〜〜

🍴
17u00
RECEPTIE & AVONDFEEST

Grand Café Lamot
Van Beethovenstraat 8/10
2800 Mechelen

♥

GRAAG EEN SEINTJE VOOR 7 MEI
KELLY VERSTRAETEN & STEFAN ACHTEN
DOKTER VAN DE PERRELEI 7 BUS 1, 2140 BORGERHOUT
KELLY: 0474 66 80 99 STEFAN: 0473 75 38 36
stefanenkelly@gmail.com
✉ of BE85 6106 7583 9006
VRIJBLIJVENDE CADEAUTIP

KELLY & STEFAN

♥

Wij gaan trouwen en nodigen u en uw partner
graag uit om erbij te zijn.

ZATERDAG
11.06.2016
· SAVE THE DATE ·

◯◯
10u30
VREDEGERECHT BORGERHOUT

Turnhoutsebaan 92, 2140 Antwerpen
Om voldoende plaats te voorzien, vragen wij u
te bevestigen of u naar de wettelijke trouw komt.

〜〜〜〜〜〜〜

♪
21u00
DANSFEEST

Grand Café Lamot
Van Beethovenstraat 8/10
2800 Mechelen

♥

GRAAG EEN SEINTJE VOOR 7 MEI
KELLY VERSTRAETEN & STEFAN ACHTEN
DOKTER VAN DE PERRELEI 7 BUS 1, 2140 BORGERHOUT
KELLY: 0474 66 80 99 STEFAN: 0473 75 38 36
stefanenkelly@gmail.com
✉ of BE85 6106 7583 9006
VRIJBLIJVENDE CADEAUTIP

Love and Liberty

Through abstract graphic language, KELLY VERSTRAETEN
reveals the secret to a strong partnership.

Every relationship is a delicate balancing act between indi-
viduality and togetherness. With this in mind, designer Kelly
Verstraeten created an invitation to her own wedding that
illustrates the give and take between partnership and inde-
pendence. Choosing abstract watercolors to best convey her
concept, Verstraeten depicts two colors symbolically moving
together but never combining to form an intermediate color.
The logo builds on the same philosophy by melding the couple's
initials without losing the form of either letter. The modern and
simple aesthetic extends to the stamp seal for the envelopes,
an illustrated map of the day's festivities, and a dinner menu. ❮

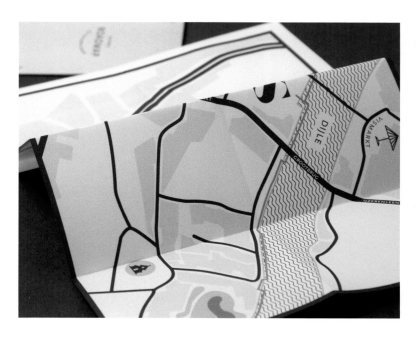

Intermingled and intertwined: two watercolors serve as a visual metaphor for the balancing act inherent in each relationship.

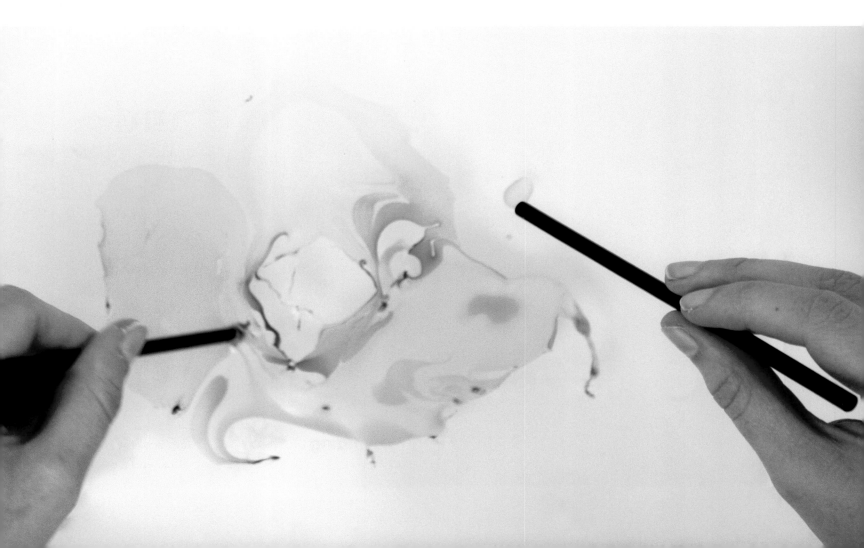

Carnival Style

KYLE WILKINSON's design for the
25th anniversary of a popular U.K. shopping mall
takes its cues from the world's biggest party.

Each year, Meadowhall Centre welcomes over 26 million visitors. As one of the U.K.'s largest shopping malls, it deserved a fitting 25th birthday celebration, complete with a bold, fun campaign that would inject a splash of color throughout the space. Kyle Wilkinson of Hacksaw was commissioned to find a design solution, which ultimately became a Carnival-style celebration featuring handmade, paper-cut illustrations to accompany a variety of Carnival-themed live acts. While the celebration has passed, the shopping continues, as does the burst of creative design energy. ❮

Two Worlds

Berlin-based studio SÜPERLEKKER's
postmarked reply cards for an international
celebration make RSVPs easy.

Süperlekker designed a double-sided card for a German-Dutch
wedding celebration that serves as both a save the date and a
reply card. The postmarked, labeled, and perforated postcards
thoughtfully leave enough space for a personal message to
the couple, building excitement for the special day. Bridging
the language gap between German and Dutch guests, all communication, including stationery, signage, and decoration,
clearly follows a two-color concept that symbolizes the varied
cultural backgrounds of the guests. The logo takes the form of
two intertwining Bs to represent the couple's initials and communicate the idea of a personal and cultural union. ❬

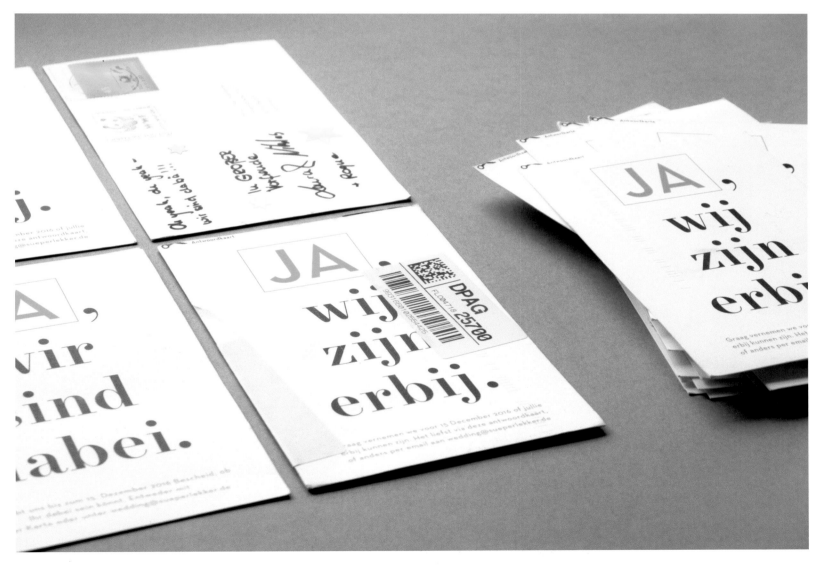

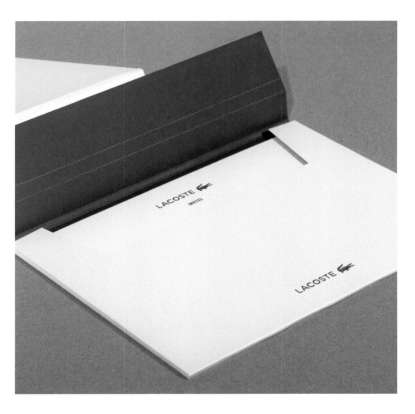

Match Point

Micro-cut invitations by **ACMÉ**
find their inspiration in Lacoste's history
on the tennis court.

Founded in 1933 by André Gillier and tennis star René Lacoste, French clothing company Lacoste made its name producing innovative tennis shirts before expanding its brand to include clothing, perfume, and accessories. The fashion house's Fall/Winter 2015 Collection draws from its roots on the court, while taking style inspiration from the primary colors, graphic patterns, and sharp edges of the 1970s and 80s. To complement this playful spirit, ACMÉ designed a set of micro-cut invitations that form a tennis court when assembled. ❮

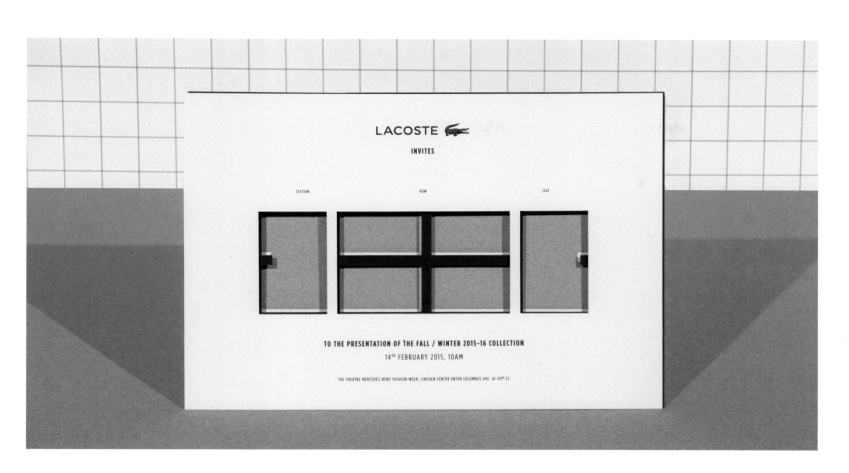

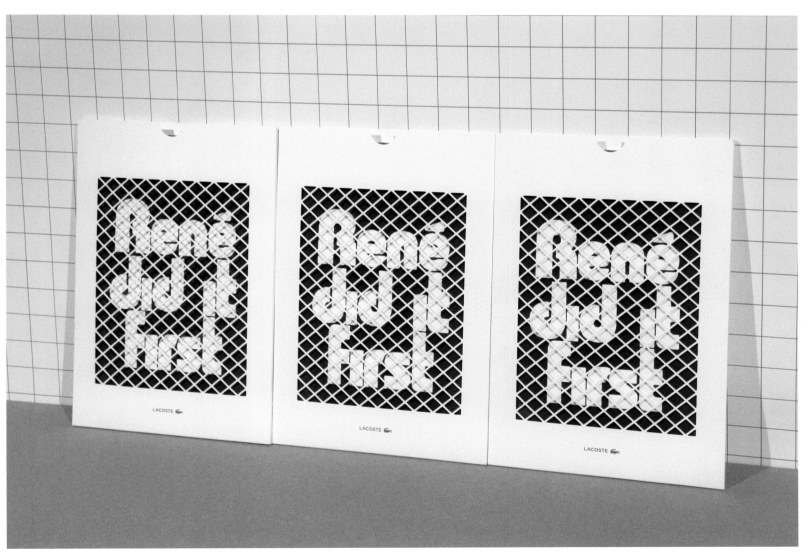

Portland

STRATEGY. CONTENT. DELIVERY.

By invitation only

Tim Allan

&

the partners
of Portland

INVITE YOU TO PORTLAND'S 15th BIRTHDAY PARTY

Thursday 20th October
from 7:30 pm
**Earth Hall,
Natural History Museum**

To RSVP, please email our events team on
RSVP@portland-communications.com or
call **0207 554 1647** for more information.

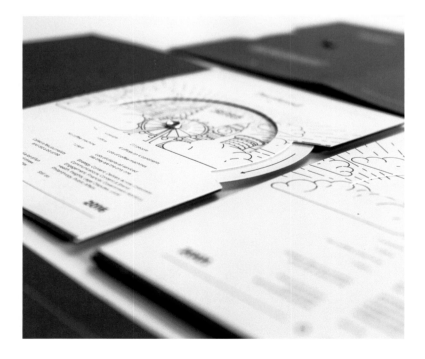

Spin the Wheel

An interactive invitation by the Content & Brand team at PORTLAND COMMUNICATIONS charts the growth of an international communications firm.

Originally founded in 2001 in London, communications consultancy Portland spent the next 15 years opening offices in Washington, DC, New York, Doha, Nairobi, and Singapore. With global teams supporting high-profile organizations, governments, and individuals in more than 85 countries, Portland wanted an invitation that celebrated their international growth. Designed by Rocco Dipoppa with the Art Direction of Natalia Zuluaga Lopez, the die-cut invitation features a spinning cardboard wheel illustrated with a skyline that highlights the landmarks of the cities where its offices can be found. ❮

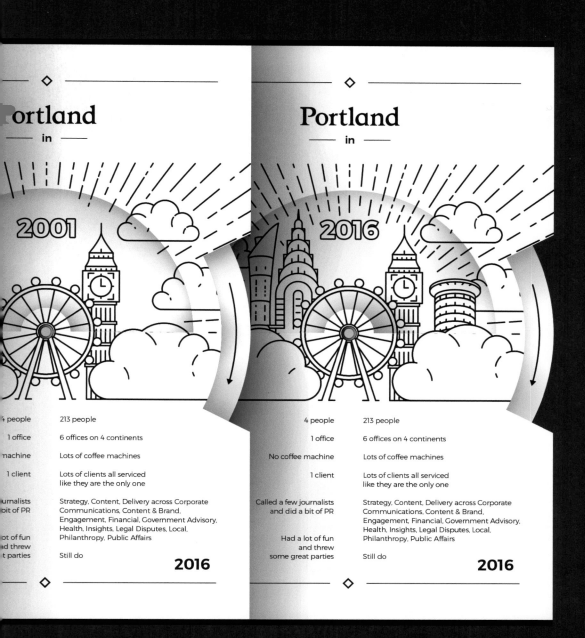

Portland
in —

2001

4 people

1 office

No coffee machine

1 client

Called a few journalists
and did a bit of PR

Had a lot of fun
and threw
some great parties

Still do

213 people

6 offices on 4 continents

Lots of coffee machines

Lots of clients all serviced
like they are the only one

Strategy, Content, Delivery across Corporate
Communications, Content & Brand,
Engagement, Financial, Government Advisory,
Health, Insights, Legal Disputes, Local,
Philanthropy, Public Affairs

2016

Portland
in —

2016

4 people

1 office

No coffee machine

1 client

Called a few journalists
and did a bit of PR

Had a lot of fun
and threw
some great parties

Still do

213 people

6 offices on 4 continents

Lots of coffee machines

Lots of clients all serviced
like they are the only one

Strategy, Content, Delivery across Corporate
Communications, Content & Brand,
Engagement, Financial, Government Advisory,
Health, Insights, Legal Disputes, Local,
Philanthropy, Public Affairs

2016

Portland
STRATEGY CONTENT DELIVERY

By invitation only
—
Tim Allan
&
the partners
of Portland

**INVITE
YOU TO
PORTLAND'S
15th BIRTHDAY
PARTY**

To RSVP, please email our events team on
RSVP@portland-communications.com or
call 0207 554 1647 for more information.

Thursday 20th October
from 7:30 pm
Earth Hall,
Natural History Museum

Not all invitations Paperlux creates
fit into a standard envelope. This is precisely
why their clients love them.

Paperlux

Hamburg [Germany]

The Hamburg-based studio Paperlux specializes in innovative corporate design for everything from invitations to identity, but the studio doesn't limit itself to working with paper. They have also created unusual and inspiring objects from wood, textiles, tiles, sandstone, and leather. When it comes to invitation design, they know that no matter what material they choose, the most important thing is that a person feels special when they receive their invitation.

As self-described material fetishists, the designers at Paperlux choose their materials with care, knowing that these anchor a design concept; without them, even the best typography and finishing techniques go to waste. As for those finishing techniques, they always tread lightly. Just because a technique is available doesn't mean it should actually be used. For Paperlux, deciding when an expensive technique is worth the investment rests on whether it helps to support the design concept—regardless of whether the budget and deadline allow for it.

An event starts the moment a guest opens an invitation, not when they walk through the door. This is Paperlux's working philosophy. Extra touches like handwriting go a

For the inauguration of
a luxury liner, Paperlux
came up with a multi-stage
invitation. The heart of
the invitation is a
linen-covered box, which
provides the view of a
maritime paper landscape.

The crank attached to the box sets waves, figurines, and vaudeville performances in motion. Paperlux developed this mechanism in collaboration with set designer Tim John. The press invitation, with the figure of a photographer, was also designed as a visual box. For the packaging, fine ropes and bowline knots were used.

long way in making an invitation feel personal, which can make all the difference in piquing the recipient's interest or influencing their decision as to whether or not to attend.

It is one thing to invite a family member to a loved one's wedding, but it is another to convince a journalist to attend an event when they receive countless invitations each year. With much experience in creating invitations for high-profile corporate clients, Paperlux is convinced that the interactive and playful ones get the biggest response.

Interactivity was the focus of their MS Europa christening invitation. The multi-stage invitation, which was increasingly built up the excitement before the event by arriving in segments. To arrive at the final concept and design, the designers did a lot of testing before presenting two working mockups to the client. One was safely within budget. The other went over budget, but was just too cool not to present. Perhaps due to the studio's practice of pitching ideas as nearly final mockups, they won the client over with the second, more expensive design, whose interactive elements set it apart.

One of the trickiest parts of the design process is meeting a client's expectations. Paperlux makes a practice of asking questions, pushing boundaries, and maintaining an element of surprise, while keeping an eye on timeline and budget. But if there is one secret they have learned, after so many years in business, it is this: always present a good idea, even if it is out of budget. One just never knows if the client will go for it. ❮

Ever since 1966, a grand jury awards a gold-plated camera to actors, musicians, and entertainers in Germany. Paperlux created the invitation for the festive gala of The Golden Kamera in 2014 using hot foil stamping, golden paper with a soft touch coating, as well as an "Ultra Black" paper.

Die 50. Verleihung der GOLDENEN KAMERA von HÖRZU am Freitag, den 27. Februar 2015

The invitation package for Daimler's World Partner Forum was inspired by three
legendary cities of the Middle Kingdom: Beijing, Xi'an and Shanghai.
It also included a uniquely cut diorama, made solely out of paper; and personalized chop-
sticks were sent over to prepare each guest for the culinary highlights.

Benjamin & Michael
invite you to celebrate their marriage
on Friday, 24 March 2017

Wedding
18.00 — 23.00
The Calyx, Royal Botanic Garden
[entry via] Palace Garden Gate
Macquarie St, Sydney
[carriages 11pm]

Discothèque
23.30 — 04.00
Tatler, 169 Darlinghurst Rd
Darlinghurst, Sydney

Please RSVP by
Wednesday, 01 March 2017
benandmikeswedding@gmail.com or 0415 774 690

Gift Registry
johnlewisgiftlist.com List N° 701285

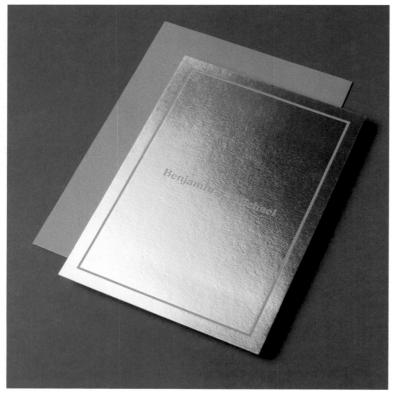

3D Spirit

Holographic wedding invitations
by **DANIEL IOANNOU** reflect the sparkling
character of a special day.

Ben and Michael's wedding was anything but the same old same old; luxe, expressive, and a true celebration of spirit, their invitations needed to reflect the personality of the event. Designer Daniel Ioannou achieved just that with an invitation: the entire front surface shines with a holographic foil that changes color in different light. This innovative printing technique, which uses a laser to print holographic images onto a thin sheet of plastic, gives a striking and vibrant character to the two-dimensional cards. An additional three sheets of G . F Smith Colorplan paper are bound together to create durable, oversized invites that double as keepsakes for guests. ❮

Benjamin ♥ Michael

Benjamin ♥ Michael

Benjamin ♥ Michael

Benjamin ♥ Michael

Benjamin ♥ Michael

Benjamin ♥ Michael

Benjamin ♥ Michael

Benja

Benjamin

Benjamin

TOGETHER WITH THEIR FAMILIES

—

JOSHUA KOH
&
DEBORAH SEOW

REQUEST THE PLEASURE OF YOUR COMPANY
TO CELEBRATE THEIR MARRIAGE

—

21.07.12

—

CEREMONY AT 9.30AM, CHIJMES HALL
GUESTS TO BE SEATED BY 9.20AM)

3.30PM, DA PAOLO ROCHEST

SAVE
THE
DATE

—

JOSHUA & DEBORAH
ARE GETTING MARRIED

21.07.12

INVITATION TO FOLLOW

J&D

Navy Minimalism

Designer GENE WANG uses letterpress printing to create standout minimalist wedding invitations.

With card-carrying minimalists as clients, designer Gene Wang knew the wedding invitations needed to be simple as well as unique. To achieve this delicate balance, Wang letterpress printed the invitations, save the dates, menus, and thank you cards with navy ink. Known for its tactile qualities, letterpress is a form of relief printing in which inked type is pressed into the paper to create a slight impression. This, in turn, creates a design element all its own: the subtle texture becomes a defining detail of the invitations without compromising their minimal essence. ❮

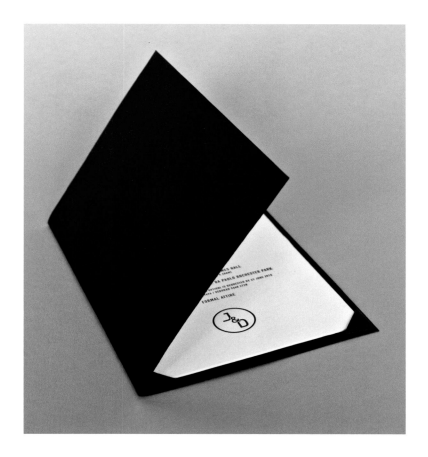

TOGETHER WITH THEIR FAMILIES

—

JOSHUA KOH
&
DEBORAH SEOW

REQUEST THE PLEASURE OF YOUR COMPANY
TO CELEBRATE THEIR MARRIAGE

—

21.07.12

CEREMONY AT 9.30AM, CHIJMES HALL
(GUESTS TO BE SEATED BY 9.20AM)

DINNER CELEBRATION AT 7.30PM, DA PAOLO ROCHESTER PARK

THE FAVOUR OF REPLY (WITH MENU OPTION) IS REQUESTED BY 21 JUNE 2012
JOSHUA 9658 9496 / DEBORAH 9648 2728

FORMAL ATTIRE

THE MENU
—
SUCCULENT CHAR GRILLED PRAWNS ON A MOUNT OF BABY
SPINACH DRIZZLED WITH HONEY MANGO DRESSING
AND TOPPED WITH FRESH AVOCADO
OR
CREAMY MUSHROOM SOUP INFUSED
WITH AROMATIC TRUFFLE OIL

—

LINGUINI WITH SHREDDED BLUE SWIMMER CRAB
SERVED IN A FLAVOURFUL TOMATO CREAM SAUCE
WITH A HINT OF VODKA

—

PLUMP BARBEQUED SEABASS WITH SMOOTH PUREED
POTATOES AND POACHED ASPARAGUS
OR
CRISP CHICKEN LEG LIGHTLY DRIZZLED WITH OLIVE OIL
AND ROASTED IN GARLIC AND ROSEMARY
SERVED ON A BED OF ROASTED POTATOES

—

TIRAMISU

—

EARL GREY TEA WEDDING CAKE
WITH SALTED CARAMEL BUTTERCREAM

One-of-a-kind

Using brush and ink, illustrator
GILL BUTTON paints every invitation to a
fashion show by hand.

Fashion designer Dries Van Noten is one of the industry's most cerebral fashion designers. Known for his bold and eccentric looks, each of his collections is a new adventure in color, pattern, and texture and is always accompanied by a dramatic runway show. For his Autumn/Winter 2016/17 show, illustrator Gill Button painted each of the 1,200 invitations by hand. Using brush and ink, her invitations portray the inspiration behind the collection, the flamboyant Italian heiress, Marchesa Casati. ❮

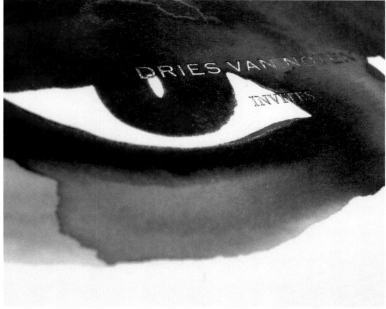

TYPE DIRECTORS CLUB

JOIN US!

Illustrative Typography

An invitation to a typography exhibit gets a custom typeface by WERNER DESIGN WERKS.

In 2014, Werner Design Werks collaborated with colleagues in the design industry to bring the annual Type Directors Club exhibition to Minneapolis. The TDC 59 show coincided with that year's AIGA National Design Conference, ensuring a large audience. The invitation for the exhibit's preview party was so well done that it drew a larger than expected turnout of over 500 designers, students, artists, and typographers from across the country. The postcard invite, which uses experimental typography that doubles as illustration, is printed on Mohawk paper by Studio on Fire. ❮

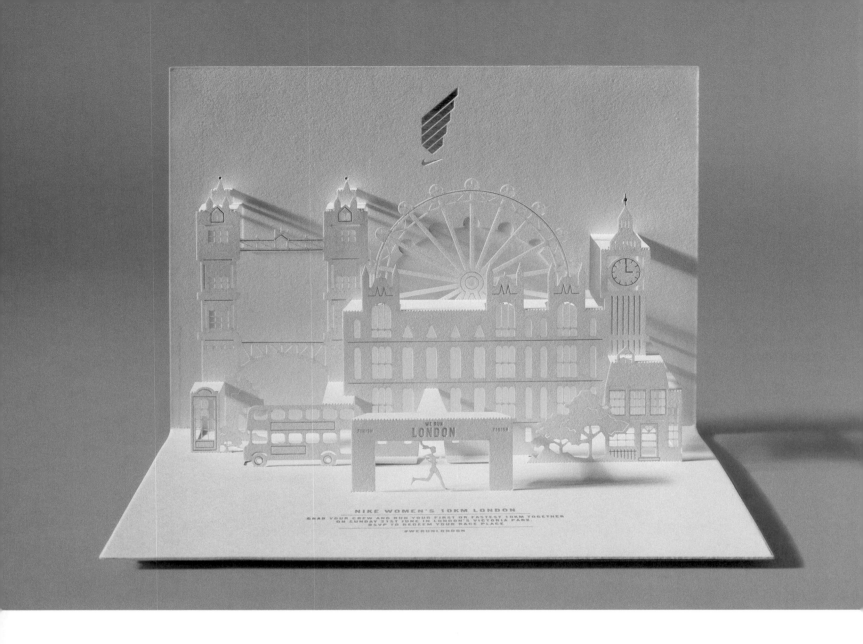

Cut from luxurious paper, London's skyline becomes a lively backdrop for the gold foil words that announce the event.

Pop-Up Story

HAPPYCENTRO hides a detailed cityscape inside a minimal design to cleverly set the path for a London race.

When London-based agency Exposure approached Happycentro to create an invitation to Nike's 2015 Women's 10K run, the designers used kirigami to add a rich layer of storytelling within an otherwise minimal design. Kirigami, which uses cut paper to make intricate designs, was the perfect counterpart to the simple materials and pared-down aesthetic of the invitation. Cut from luxurious Materica paper by Fedrigoni, London's skyline becomes a lively backdrop for the minimal words that announce the event. The final piece contains six folded laser-cut layers with gold foil highlights inside a 180 + 360 gsm envelope. ❮

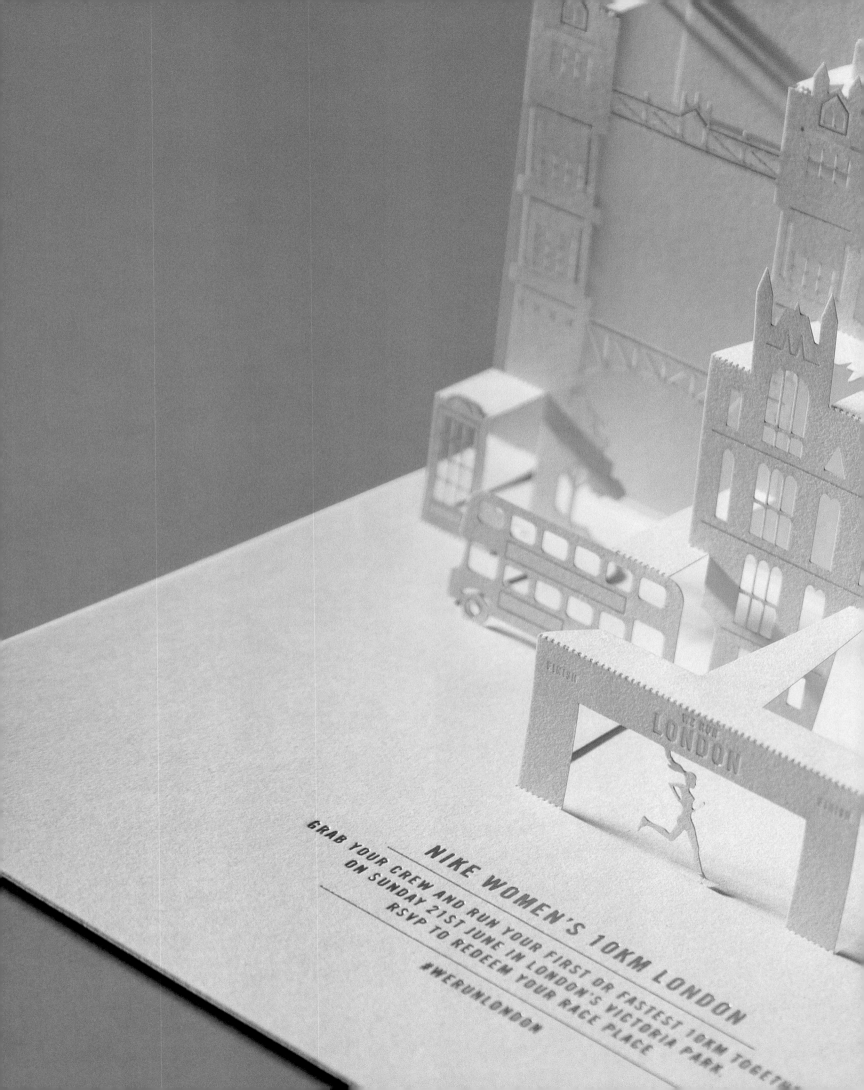

WE RUN LONDON

NIKE WOMEN'S 10KM LONDON

GRAB YOUR CREW AND RUN YOUR FIRST OR FASTEST 10KM TOGETHER
ON SUNDAY 21ST JUNE IN LONDON'S VICTORIA PARK.
RSVP TO REDEEM YOUR RACE PLACE

#WERUNLONDON

It was a long process from the first rough tests to the final delivery of the invitations. The team at Happycentro designed the skyline, tested the mechanism of the six different foldable layers, laser cut all the invitations, applied golden foil for architecture details and texts, and hand-mounted each kirigami to its cover, one by one.

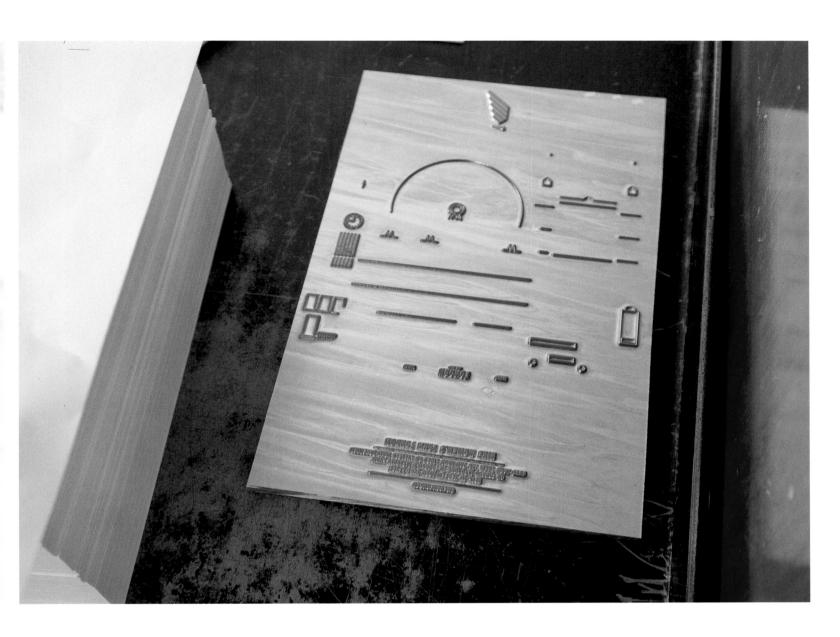

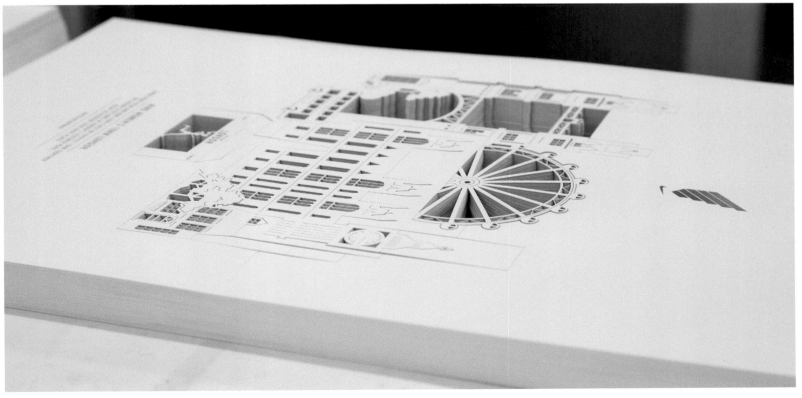

Labor of Love

ELENA BULAY brings a fresh look
to a modern-day wedding invitation, using
an old-world printing technique.

Designer Elena Bulay's contribution to her friend's wedding did not just end with stunning invitation design; her vision also included linocut printing, the design carved into a block of linoleum used to print each card by hand. The technique creates a charmingly simple, high-contrast look—the perfect complement to Bulay's botanical-themed drawings. The illustrations adorn each piece of a three-part invitation suite: the larger main card announces the date and the couple's names, while a smaller card includes the time and location of the event; and the third element, a small apple, bears the name of the guest. Green and brown raffia tie all three together to create an elegant handmade invitation. ❮

The technique creates a charmingly simple, high-contrast look— the perfect complement to Bulay's botanical-themed drawings.

46

All Things Tactile

MOODLEY BRAND IDENTITY's comprehensive corporate design helps build an innovative business.

Moodley Brand Identity has been with Martina Sperl since she founded her modern upholstery business, fashioning everything from her business cards to signage and tags. Sperl has made significant waves, approaching the upholstery business by entirely rethinking it. The award-winning corporate design not only highlights her personality, but also introduces the personality of her furniture: true works of craftsmanship revitalized with a love for detail. For her store's grand opening, the invitations needed to make a splash. So the agency used fabric samples as a backdrop for the sleek announcements, capturing the essence of Sperl's business and its tactile offerings. ❮

5424 HUDSON AVE
OKLAHOMA CITY, OK 73118

OTIS BELVINS
7401 N WALKER
OKLAHOMA CITY, OK 73162

PRESORTED
FIRST-CLASS MAIL
US POSTAGE
PAID
ZIP CODE 97206
PERMIT NO. 3946

Camera Obscura

TAYLOR HALE's interactive exhibition invitation turns invitees into exhibitors.

Created as both the invitation to, and the content of, a blind photography exhibit at an Oklahoma City university, designer Taylor Hale's award-winning 3D camera obscura is a laser-cut invitation that can be delivered by mail or hand. The invitation includes instructions for the invitee on how to use the one-exposure camera. After making an image with their camera/invitation, the recipient then returns it to the sender. After all of the images are returned, the sender exhibits them to the public. ❮

Sometimes an invitation is more than a formal gesture, and it smoothly becomes part of the event itself.

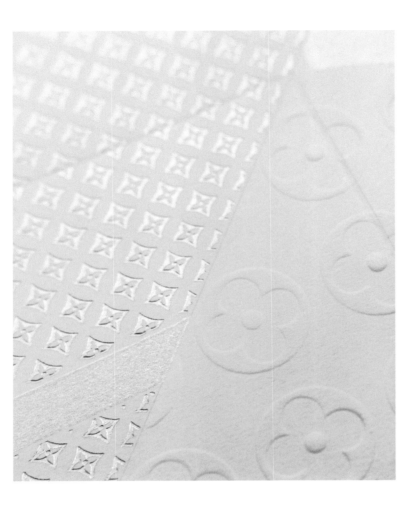

Paper Sculptures

Luscious printing on sheets of origami paper defines these sculptural invitations by HAPPYCENTRO.

When asked to design and produce the invitation for the opening of a Louis Vuitton store in Osaka, Japan, designer Federico Galvani of Happycentro knew he wanted to create a paper object. Combining the shape, precision, and expressive qualities of origami with sophisticated printing techniques proved an effective way to communicate the character of the event. The final piece uses a mixture of transparent, silver mat and pearl foils with relief printing on a thin sheet of paper, creating a flat sheet that is valley-folded to hold a smaller sheet of assembly directions. ❮

The talented illustrator <u>Lize-Marie Dreyer</u>
seeks to explore the magic of imagination in her
unique custom-made designs.

Aurora Creative Studio

Cape Town [South Africa]

Lize-Marie Dreyer, the award-winning designer and illustrator behind Aurora Creative Studio, believes that good invitation design is comparable to a good movie trailer: it quickly tells a story in a way that captivates an audience and leaves them excited to see what will happen next. As someone who delights in receiving beautifully crafted invitations herself, Dreyer sets the bar high with her work, designing the kinds of invitations that she would also love to receive.

If anything characterizes Dreyer's style and sets it apart, it is a meticulous attention to detail. Inspired by her clients and their stories, it is the small details that are paramount. You will never see her using templates or turning her custom invitations into templates, even though she is often asked for a reproduction of a past design. While it would be an easy thing to do as a designer, she politely declines, as it contradicts her entire process and

Finding inspiration in the colorful birds and botanicals that inhabit South Africa's vast savannas, Lize-Marie Dreyer created a series of illustrations that became the central theme of the stationery.

ASHLEY'S PAMPER PARTY

5TH MARCH 2016

What is your favorite memory of us?

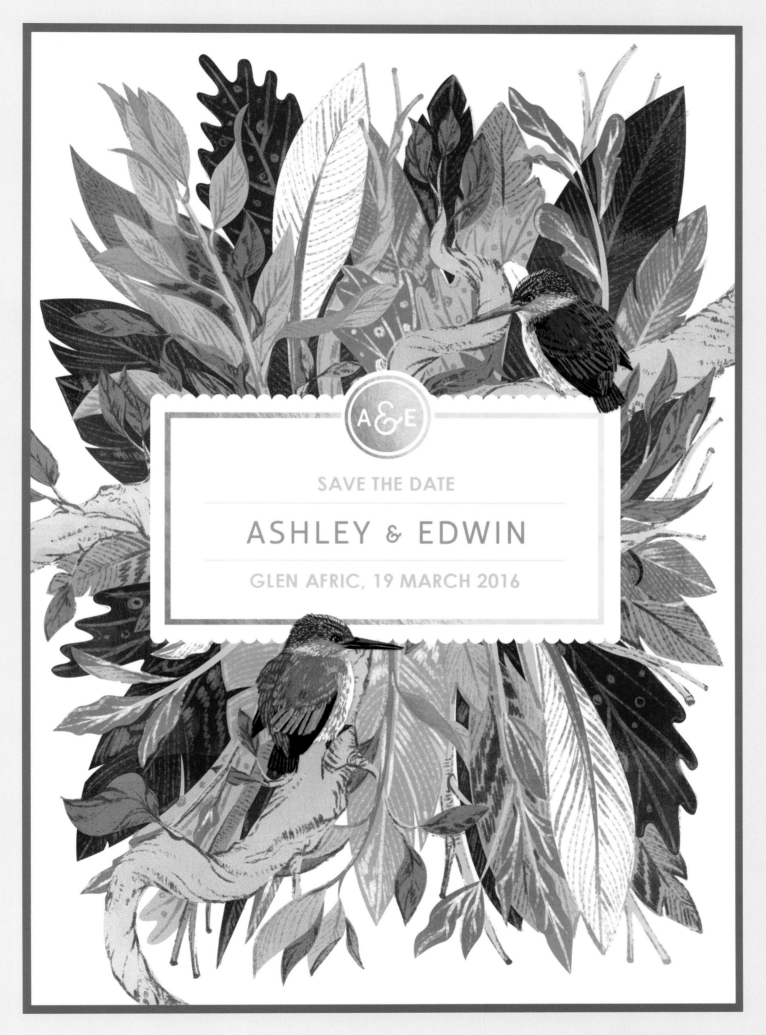

SAVE THE DATE

ASHLEY & EDWIN

GLEN AFRIC, 19 MARCH 2016

First Lize-Marie Dreyer makes sketches and explores some initial color palette options, based on her conversations with the client. Once they approve the direction, she takes the idea into Illustrator for shapes and color mapping, then Photoshop for detailed work, and finally InDesign where she finalizes the layout and information.

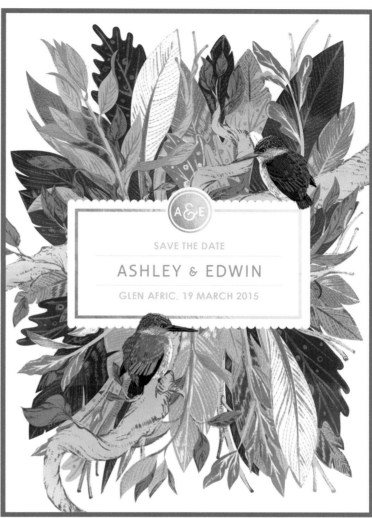

SAVE THE DATE

ASHLEY & EDWIN

GLEN AFRIC, 19 MARCH 2015

philosophy. Her stationery sets are developed by listening to the unique story that each and every couple has to tell. And with so many other elements of the wedding industry being customized at high cost, Dreyer believes that each invitation should be customized as well.

A prolific illustrator, Dreyer has a dexterous ability to switch between styles, which serves her well as a stationery designer. She works primarily in two different styles: one is more traditional, and the other has a more geometric, digital quality. Switching between the two not only opens up more opportunities, but is also creatively satisfying. It keeps things fresh and inspiring, and gives her clients a wider range of possibilities.

Having a background in both design and illustration allows Dreyer to enter territory that would be off-limits to someone with a narrower skill set. Her ability to translate the brief for each project into a tangible object with a custom visual language is a rare ability. Although each invitation is unique, her average turnaround time for a save the

date and invitation tends to be two to three weeks. During this time, she makes sketches and some initial color palette options based on her conversations with the couple. Once they approve the direction, she takes the idea into Adobe Illustrator for shapes and color mapping, then Photoshop for detailed work, and finally InDesign to finish off the layout.

Ultimately, the level of detail, time, and effort that Dreyer puts into her work results in an invitation that creates excitement leading up to a couple's wedding day. It is no surprise that Dreyer's clients often turn their invitations into a piece of wall art, a meaningful keepsake that can be framed and displayed long after the event. ‹

Taking her inspiration from all of the locations that shaped the couple into who they are today, she infused each element with the visual language of travel; the order of ceremonies, menus, and thank you cards are designed to look like boarding passes, passports, and postcards.

Rendered
in a flat design
style that is
reminiscent of
infographics,
each piece
is playful,
but also infor-
mative.

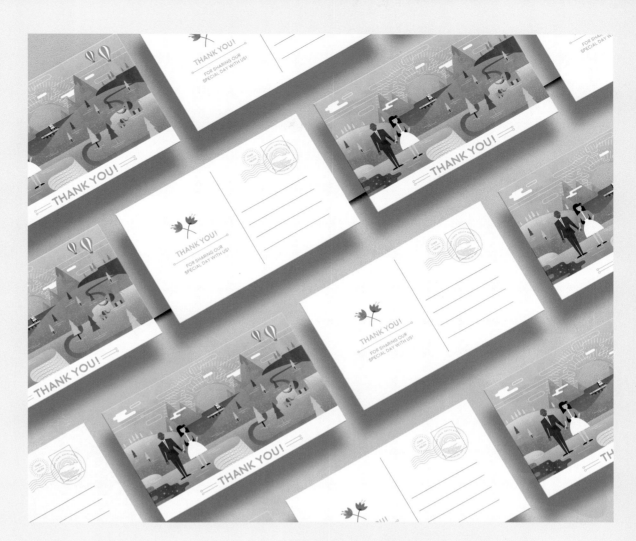

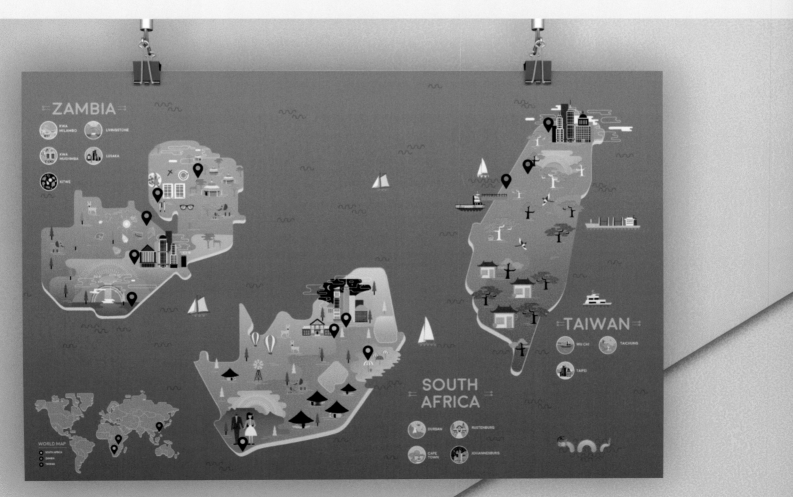

CHAD & HELEN

CAPE TOWN, SOUTH AFRICA

17TH DECEMBER 2016

FIRST CLASS
TICKET

NUMBER
17.12.16

JOHANNESBURG

SEAT
1A

FLIGHT   17.12
GATE   C 16
TAG US   #CHADHELENWEDDING

ADMIT ONE

BOARDING PASS

Left panel:
...DING
...RAM

...00 PM
...EDDING
...REMONY

...M
...G OF THE
...AGE REGISTER

5.30 PM
PRE-DINNER
DRINKS &
LIGHT
SNACKS

...00 PM
...INNER

9.00 PM
DESSERT

Right panel:
W...
PR...

3.30 PM
GUESTS TO
BE SEATED

5.00 PM
PICTURES
WITH FAM...
AND FRIEN...

9.3...
DA...

CHAD
&
HELEN

CAPE TOWN, SOUTH AFRICA
17TH DECEMBER 2016

FIRST CLASS
TICKET

NUMBER
17.12.16

JOHANNESBURG

SEAT
1B

FLIGHT   17.12
GATE   C 16
TAG US   #CHADHELENWEDDING

ADMIT ONE

BOARDING PASS

वक्रतुण्ड महाकाय सूर्यकोटि समप्रभ निर्विघ्नं कुरु मे देव सर्वकार्येषु सर्वदा ॥

Modern Mythology

Traditional symbolism meets contemporary design in an Indian wedding invitation by **NITEESH YADAV**.

When Prateek and Deepti commissioned Niteesh Yadav to design their wedding invitations, they asked for a contemporary interpretation of traditional Indian invitations, which typically feature references to mythology. The final piece incorporates Lord Ganesha, the remover of disruption and disorder in Hindu mythology, into a modern and playful design. Using a mix of digital and screen printing techniques, the invite was rendered on custom-made paper and enclosed in a custom red envelope. ❮

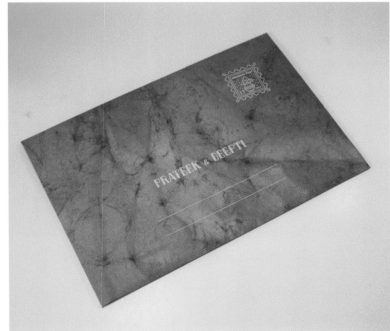

Tenerife Dreaming

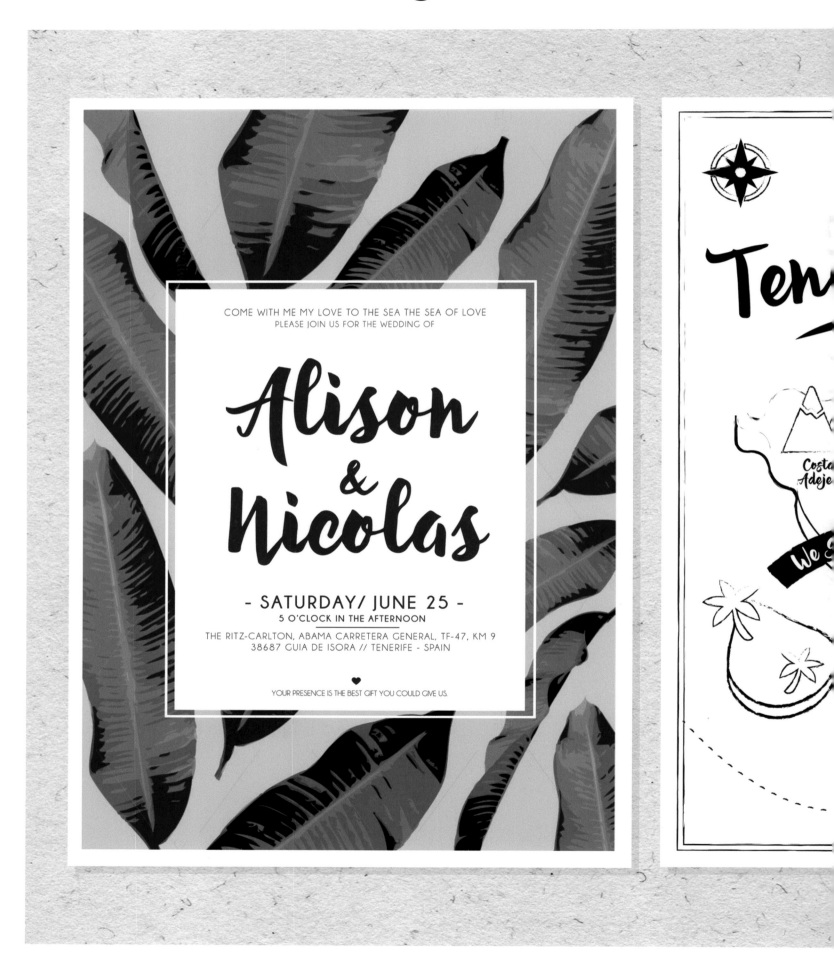

COME WITH ME MY LOVE TO THE SEA THE SEA OF LOVE
PLEASE JOIN US FOR THE WEDDING OF

Alison
&
Nicolas

- SATURDAY/ JUNE 25 -

5 O'CLOCK IN THE AFTERNOON

THE RITZ-CARLTON, ABAMA CARRETERA GENERAL, TF-47, KM 9
38687 GUIA DE ISORA // TENERIFE - SPAIN

♥

YOUR PRESENCE IS THE BEST GIFT YOU COULD GIVE US.

Ideally, the look and feel of the invitation reflects the character of the actual event. With her illustrations, SALOMÉ GAUTIER has perfectly set the tone for a laid back yet stylish beach wedding.

Santa Cruz

Teide 3718

Reina Sofia

SCHEDULE SATURDAY, JUNE 25

♥ 5PM : CEREMONY – PIER

🍸 6PM : COCKTAIL – BEACH CLUB

🍴 8.30PM : DINNER – EL

🎈 11PM : BEACH PARTY

SUNDAY, JUNE 26

🥐 9 AM : BREAKFAST – LA

Alison & Nicolas

DRESS CODE : BEACH

Elle Robe d'été décontractée, courte ou longue, tons rose, fuchsia, corail, orange,... PAS de robe de cocktail.

Il Chemise blanche, bermuda beige, chaussures style mocassins/ basket en toile,... PAS de cravate, de chaussures de costume, de shorts à poches ni de tongs.

N'OUBLIEZ PAS L'ESSENTIEL

AEROPORTS & RESERVATION VOL

✈

Tenerife Sud - Reina Sofia. Veuillez réserver votre vol par vos propres moyens. Pour éviter tout risque de retard le jour du mariage, nous vous invitons à arriver à Tenerife le vendredi 24 juin.

Réservation Chambres The Ritz-Carlton, Abama
Nous avons pré-réservé des chambres Deluxe avec un tarif spécial. Veuillez donc effectuer la réservation de votre chambre en direct avec l'hôtel via le lien suivant ou par téléphone en indiquant le Group Code « QAVA».

Les personnes souhaitant prolonger leur séjour à l'hôtel bénéficieront du tarif spécial pendant 5 jours après le mariage. Profitez !

https://reservations.ritzcarlton.com/ritz/reservation/availability.mi?propertyCode=TFSRZ

Pour les personnes souhaitant réserver une chambre de catégorie supérieure ou pour toute information concernant la réservation veuillez contacter

irene.couso@ritzcarlton.com

Rural Elegance

Vintage-inspired invites by
DANIEL IOANNOU offer a vivid preview of a
Californian destination wedding.

With a weekend wedding celebration planned at a charming rural ranch in California's Chileno Valley, Adam and Dorian wanted their invitations to introduce the unique location and special event to their guests. Designer Daniel Ioannou's fresh and exciting stationery reflects not only the landscape surrounding the ceremony, but also the style of the ranch's interior and the elegant feel of the weekend. Within meticulously calligraphed luxe cream envelopes, guests received invitations set in muted color palettes to evoke the rolling green hills of the valley. The various botanical illustrations on the invitations, fact sheets, and thank you cards echo the venue's vintage-style decor. ❮

YOU'RE INVITED

A+D

A+D

Adam Kuperman + Dorian Ferlauto together with their
families invite you to attend their wedding weekend.

SATURDAY JUNE 27TH 2015 AT 4 O'CLOCK

CHILENO VALLEY RANCH
5105 Chileno Valley Rd, Petaluma, CA 94952

TRANSPORTATION
Shuttles leaving from Waterfront Hotel
@ 2pm Returning at 9pm + 10pm

DRESS
Formal. We will be walking on grass and gravel

RÉPONDEZ S'IL VOUS PLAÎT
by May 31st 2015, to adam.kuperman@gmail.com

6.26.15	6.28.15
REHEARSAL DINNER	**SUNDAY BRUNCH**
OAKLAND, CA	**OAKLAND, CA**
Hosted: By Marcie Morrison	Hosted: By Katherine Ferlauto

ALL THE FACTS

A+D

A+D

WHERE TO STAY
Waterfront Hotel
Jack London Square
10 Washington St. Oakland, CA
Kuperman / Ferlauto Block

**WEDDING DAY
TRANSPORTATION**
We are whisking you away to wine
country with shuttles leaving from the
Waterfront Hotel at 2pm
Returning at 9pm and 10pm

DRESS
Formal. We will be outdoors, so be
ready for sun, gravel and grass

TRANSPORTATION
BART from airport to hotel
Ferry To SF located in Jack London

GETTING AROUND TOWN
Download the Lyft or Uber apps
on your phone for convenient
in-town transportation

WHAT TO DO
Friday Farmers Market
9-2pm 9th and Broadway

Sunday Farmers Market
9-2pm Jack London Square

COFFEE
Blue Bottle Coffee
300 Webster St

LIBATIONS
The Trappist - 460 8th St.
Beer Revolution - 464 3rd St.

WHERE TO EXPLORE
Take The Ferry To SF

Old Oakland
*Just up the street with many
options for food and drink.*

China Town
*Right around the corner
and offers some very authentic
cultural experiences.*

VISIT OUR WEDDING WEBSITE FOR ALL THE DETAILS
ADAMPLUSDORIAN.COM

Inspired by the German poster artist Ludwig Hohlwein, Kyoto-based
STUDIO-TAKEUMA creates witty invites for various weddings.

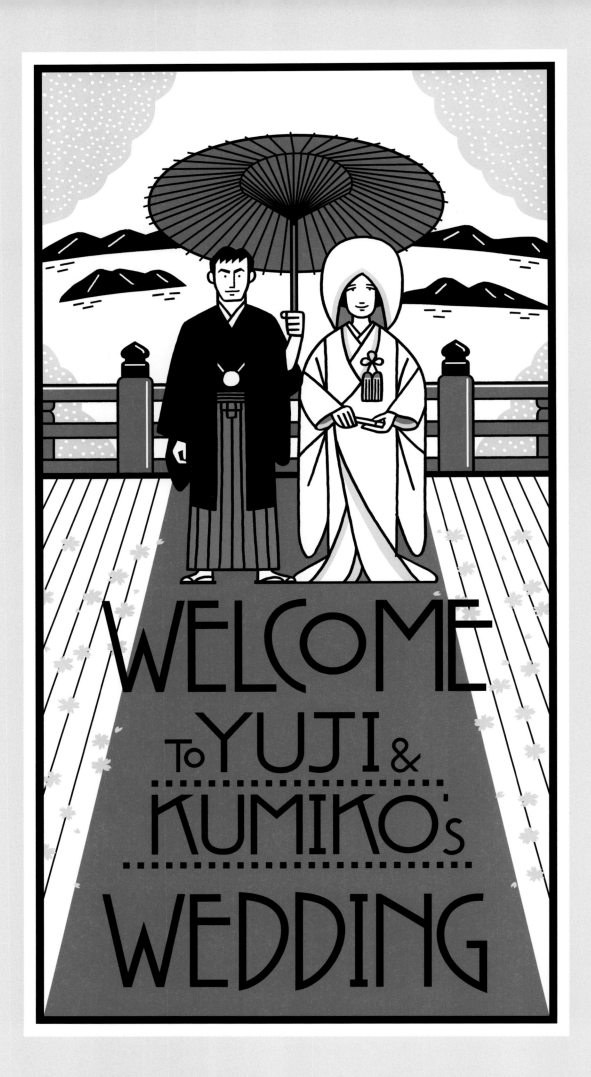

La ceremonia civil se
celebrará a las 12:15 H.
en la Junta Municipal
de Retiro.

Lo celebraremos con un
banquete vegetariano
en la Finca Normande-
Ondarreta.

Se ruega confirmación.
· Isabel: 617 143 590
· Carlos: 657 662 633

Four-Legged Family

TERESA BELLÓN's animal-loving clients
requested that she include their dog and three cats
into an illustrated wedding invitation.

AVDA. CIUDAD DE BARCELONA

→ AVDA. CIUDAD DE BARCELONA 162

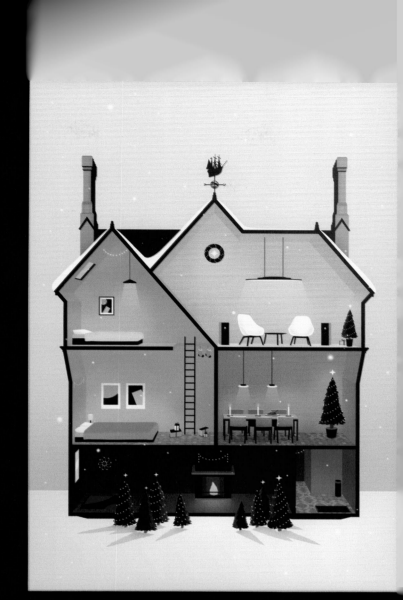

Slight of Hand

A vintage printing technique adds 3D views to this holiday invitation by THOMAS DANTHONY.

Founded in 1884 by Arthur Liberty, Liberty London subsequently grew into an iconic store and fashion house known for its focus on pattern and design. In keeping with its tradition of working in close collaboration with designers, Liberty partnered with French-born, London-based artist Thomas Danthony to create a Christmas press day invitation. Known for his bold, narrative imagery, Danthony created two illustrations for the front of the stationery—an interior and an exterior view of Liberty's iconic building. The two images are combined using lenticular printing, which allows the recipient to alternate between views by tilting the card back and forth. ❮

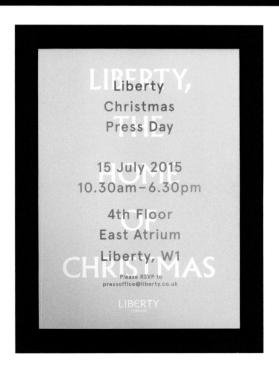

Liberty,
Christmas
Press Day

15 July 2015
10.30am – 6.30pm

4th Floor
East Atrium
Liberty, W1

Please RSVP to
pressoffice@liberty.co.uk

LIBERTY
LONDON

王仕超

廖郁欣

74

Seal of Approval

Designer **WANG SHI-CHAO** puts a modern twist on traditional Chinese seals for his own wedding invitation.

Taiwanese designer Wang Shi-Chao took the occasion of his own wedding to create an invitation that combines the art of traditional Chinese seals with modern minimalism. Typically, the Chinese seal would contain the first names of the bride and groom, but Wang's concept combines his first initial together with that of his wife, Hikki's. By combining the two strokes of the letters into one seal, their union is symbolized across the invitation set. The bold pink and blue color palette gives the invitations a contemporary feel, while gold foil printing delicately offsets the more subtle kraft paper envelopes. ‹

Amanda

FIRST COURSE
Choice of
HOUSE CURED DUCK PROSCIUTT...
Mixed Greens, Pecorino, Strawberries, Aged Balsamic, Shave...

GRILLED ASPARAGUS SALAD
Egg Dressing, Shaved Vegetables, Herbs and Lett...

SECOND COURSE
Choice of
BEEF DUO
Seared Tenderloin and Braised Short Ribs, Carrot Purée, M...
Bacon Marmalade, Broccoli Rabe and Bordelaise S...

OLIVE OIL POACHED ORGANIC SALM...
Beluga Lentils, Cauliflower, Kale

DESSERT
Choice of
EXOTIC VACHERIN
Macerated Pineapple, Mango, Kiwi, Mojito Foam...
Coconut Custard, Tropical Sorbet

PRALINE MILK CHOCOLATE BAR...
Praline-Milk Chocolate Mousse, Toffee Popcorn...
Sesame Gelato, Frangelico Caramel

Amanda

FIRST COURSE
ROASTED BEET SALAD
Cherry Vinaigrette, Candied Walnuts,
Edgwick Farm Goat Cheese, Radish

SECOND COURSE
RACK OF LAMB
Farro Grain, Swiss Chard, Spring Onion,
Salsa Verde, Red Wine Jus

DESSERT COURSE
LEMON OLIVE OIL TART
Toasted Marshmallow, Strawberry Elderflower Sorbet,
Marco Polo Granité, Yuzu Foam

WEDD...

THE CELEBRATION A...
THE MARR...

Amanda No...
AND
Jake Davi...

AUGUST 2...

1

The New York-based design studio **FOURTEEN-FORTY** is renowned for their custom-made calligraphy invitations.
To add an extra touch of elegance to this particular design, an extra seal was created.

AUGUST 27, 2016

WELCOME!
We are thrilled you are here, let's celebrate!
Love,
Amanda & Jake

SCHEDULE OF EVENTS

Glenmere Mansion
634 Pine Hill Road, Chester New York

WEDDING CEREMONY	COCKTAILS	DINNER & DANCING	AFTER PARTY	BRUNCH
5:00 pm, Saturday *In the Meadow*	6:00 pm, Saturday *Cortile and Living Room*	7:30 pm, Saturday *Lakeside Terrace*	11:30 pm - 2:30 am Saturday *Formal Gardens*	9:00 am - 11:00 am Sunday *Glenmere Mansion*

TRANSPORTATION
PICK-UP TIMES FOR CEREMONY, CELEBRATION AND BRUNCH

SATURDAY
Buses depart Holiday Inn at 4:30 pm and at 5:00 pm
for the Ceremony at Glenmere. Buses depart
at Glenmere starting at 11:00 pm with continuing
departures every 30 minutes ending at 2:45 am.

SUNDAY
Bus departs Holiday Inn at 8:30 am for the
Brunch at Glenmere. Bus departs Glenmere at
11:00 am for return to Holiday Inn.

Amanda + Jake
AUGUST 27, 2016

anda Siebert

Jake Skinner

"We always look for ways to add an extra something special to wedding invitation suites, whether it is a wax seal, a map, or calligraphy."

FOURTEEN-FORTY

200 EAST 15TH STREET
APARTMENT 12E
NEW YORK, NEW YORK 10003

"*Love each other
as I have loved you*"
– JOHN 15:12

TINA & BRETT
AUGUST 8, 2015
CHURCH OF THE MESSIAH • RHINEBECK, NEW YORK

"*And now
here is my secret,
a very simple secret.
It is only with the
heart that one
can see rightly:
what is essential
is invisible
to the eye.*"

ANTOINE DE SAINT-EXUPÉRY, THE LITTLE PRINCE

TOGETHER WITH THEIR PARENTS

Tina Eunseon Chang
AND
Brett Lawrence Gaudin

REQUEST THE PLEASURE OF YOUR COMPANY
AT THE CELEBRATION OF THEIR MARRIAGE

, SATURDAY, THE EIGHTH OF AUGUST
TWO THOUSAND FIFTEEN
AT HALF PAST THREE IN THE AFTERNOON

THE CHURCH OF THE MESSIAH
RHINEBECK, NEW YORK

· · · · · · · · · · · · · · · · · · · ·

COCKTAIL HOUR AND RECEPTION
TO IMMEDIATELY FOLLOW

GRASMERE FARM • RHINEBECK, NEW YORK
COCKTAIL ATTIRE

· · · · · · · · · · · · · · · · · · · ·

ARE YOU IN?
PLEASE RESPOND ON OR BEFORE JULY 11, 2015

WHEN TINA AND BRETT _____ DOWN
                                    (VERB)
THE _____ ON AUGUST 8TH,
            (NOUN)
_____ _____ BE THERE TO
    (YOUR NAME/S)   (WILL / WILL NOT)
_____ THEM. I'M / WE'RE SO _____
        (VERB)   (ADJECTIVE)
FOR TINA AND BRETT, AND CAN'T WAIT TO SEE THEM
_____ AT THE WEDDING. MY ADVICE TO
        (VERB)
THE NEWLY-WEDS IS TO MAKE SURE TO ALWAYS
_____ AS MUCH AS
    (ANYTHING GOES)
POSSIBLE. I / WE WISH THEM A LIFETIME OF
HAPPINESS AND _____
                    (ANYTHING GOES)
                    NUMBER ATTENDING _____

TINA & BRETT
200 EAST 15TH STREET
APARTMENT 12E
NEW YORK, NEW YORK
10003

Featuring a distinctive floral style,
Venamour offers semi-custom wedding ephemera that are
meant to leave a lasting first impression.

Venamour

New York City [USA]

When designer Lisa Hedge saw her parents' wedding invitation for the first time, she was struck by the sweet simplicity of the folded card, with its delicate line work on the front and traditional wording on the interior. It is still her go-to when she needs a reminder that tradition can help show us how to invent the present. It is a take on the creative process that is visible in her own studio, Venamour, where she has carved out a niche in the world of wedding stationery by offering semi-custom ephemera that draw on a unique combination of traditional and contemporary influences.

Floral motifs are a central design element in Venamour's work. It is a direction that came about naturally as Hedge found the choice of wedding flowers at the center of understanding her clients' sensibilities—how certain flowers might translate into the color, shape, and texture of a couple's invitations. Her artful, unexpected approach, which combines floral collages

"The goal was to create a polished design aesthetic that doesn't feel overtly romantic, whimsical, or traditional."

LISA HEDGE

CAELIA & LUKE
127 PIERREPONT STREET NO. 9A
BROOKLYN, NEW YORK 11201

EMMA AND JONATHAN ANDREWS
12 BLUE JAY DRIVE
CONCORD, MASSACHUSETTS 01742

R . S . V . P .

"What we do seems to tie into the attitude that is emerging in all other visual
aspects of weddings, with less concern for overly cohesive wedding schemes, and more interest
in unexpected and mismatched elements—from loose and natural bouquets and discoordinated
bridesmaid dresses to non-traditional venues," says Lisa Hedge.

with the typographic languages of editorial design and luxury branding, resonates with her clients and reveals an underserved market where Venamour ultimately found its home. By creating a business that focused on a polished design aesthetic, Hedge spearheaded a growing trend in the wedding industry that embraces the unusual instead of the overly coordinated.

The result is Venamour's instantly recognizable stationery that delivers carefully curated aesthetics instead of template-heavy designs, as well as one-on-one guidance along the way. The studio's refined process starts with the client choosing between three collections that revolve around a different botanical motif. From there, the client picks a style and treatment of the artwork that can be used in various ways—as a delicate framing element or

as a bold, all-over print—on all materials. Once the floral aspect of the design is in place, Hedge helps clients navigate the selection of a typestyle, layout, envelope color, and addressing style, as well as language that will capture the tone and mood of the event. Ultimately, these choices produce a unique result.

Over the years, Venamour has also used printing as a means of expression, whether in taking advantage of the range of possibilities offered by high-end digital presses or by embracing the old-world charm of letterpress. As her studio grows and evolves, Hedge continues to experiment with creative direction and to educate herself in finishing techniques that can best infuse the work with depth—a process allowing her to play with tradition in order to create something completely new. ‹

Borrowing the formal language of editorial design and some elements from luxury branding, Venamour has achieved a distinct style, which feels contemporary, elegant, and unmistakingly feminine at the same time.

PLEASE JOIN US ON

THE TWELFTH OF
SEPTEMBER,
TWENTY FIFTEEN
AT FOUR O'CLOCK IN
THE AFTERNOON
TO CELEBRATE THE
WEDDING OF
EVELYN ANDREWS
AND JAMES WRIGHT

AN INTIMATE CEREMONY
12 BLUE JAY DRIVE, CONCORD, MASSACHUSETTS
—
RECEPTION TO FOLLOW

&THE BEACH
BOOKSTORE
AMSTERDAM
IT'S A WRAP
invitation & wrapping
paper in one!
11.12
2014
VIEREN
GARAGE
NOTWEG
NOTWEG 38
DRESSCODE
ROOD & UITBUNDIG

Beste Deelnemers,
Samenwerkings en Netwerk partners,

Het is weer een fantastisch jaar geweest en
Osdorp is hot en happening!

Vanaf mei dit jaar is THE
LOCKWOOD

samenwerking met theatermaker Aldo Brinkhof
DJ Mitchell LC Yard zorgt voor het
vuurwerk en natuurl
echte

It's a Wrap!

MARTA VELUDO's holiday party invite finds a
second life as custom gift wrap.

Running with the idea that two is better than one, designer
Marta Veludo created a holiday party invitation for the
Bookstore Foundation, its oversized format cleverly doubling
as a sheet of wrapping paper. Riso printed in two colors on
an A3 sheet of paper, the invitation incorporates a mash up of
ten patterns, which gives the design a playful wrapping-paper
option. Printed in an edition of 150, each invitation is one-of-a-
kind and is delivered in a wrapped tube. ❮

Invitation to Interact

ASTRID ORTIZ's boldly patterned invitation encourages attendees to socialize upon arrival.

Fashion brand Desigual is all about bold, fun pattern combinations. Astrid Ortiz's invitation design for its Say Something Nice Spring/Summer 2015 Collection collection embodies this aesthetic attitude with audacious patterns and colors—and an unusual twist. Instead of simply informing recipients about the event's time and place, it invites them to say something nice to each other once they arrive. Using an assortment of stickers that contain a variety of compliments, guests can stick nice words on one another to start a conversation, enhancing the social experience of the event. ❮

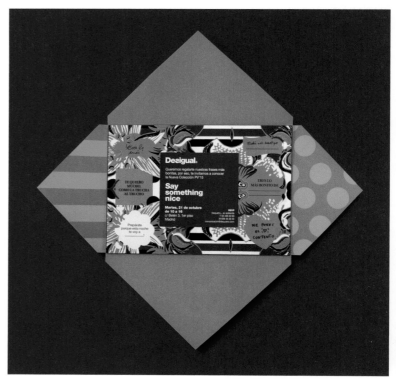

Instead of simply informing recipients about the event's time and place, this invite inspires them to say something nice to each other once they arrive.

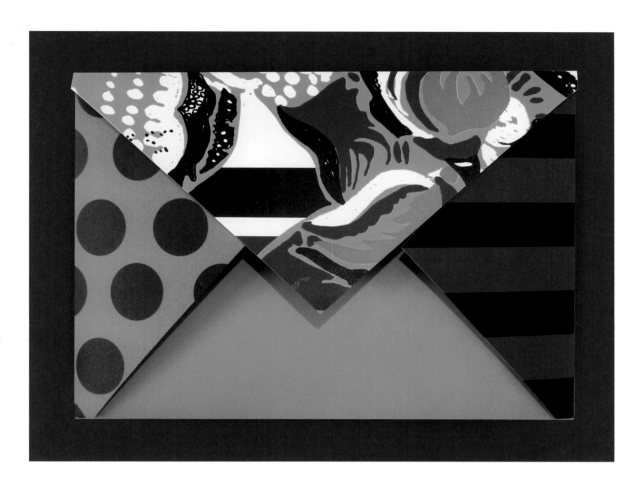

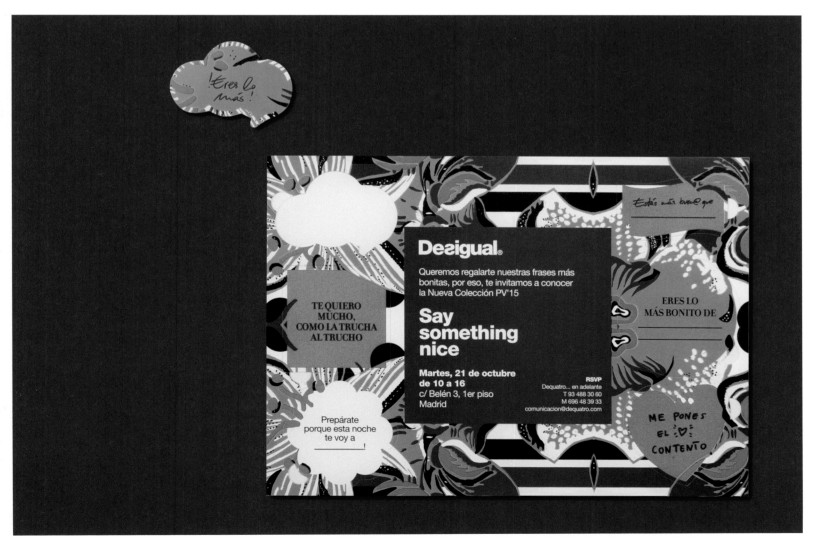

17TH JULY 2014 / 6.30 - 9.00PM
YOU ARE INVITED TO EXPLORE
THE CIVIC GALLERY, BARNSLEY, S70 2HZ
ENLIGHTENED
PLEASE RSVP TO RSVP@ENLIGHTENEDLASER.COM
WE WOULD LOVE YOU TO JOIN US FOR THE
ENLIGHTENED - AN EXHIBITION

Laser Sharp

KYLE WILKINSON's laser-engraved invitation for an innovative exhibition is a work of art itself.

Originally conceived as an art exhibition, *Enlightened* collected the work of U.K.-based designers and creatives exploring the use of lasers in design. Together, their work showcases the range of possibilities in laser cutting and engraving and educates the public on the latest laser technology. For the event, Kyle Wilkinson created a laser-engraved invitation that could have been a piece in the show. Used with a variety of materials, this technique leaves a mark by utilizing the high heat from the laser to vaporize the surface. ‹

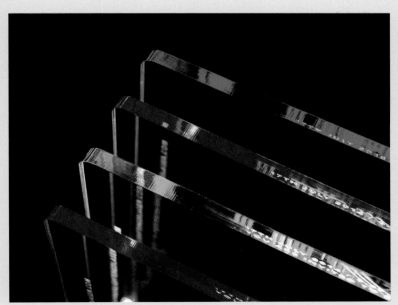

80s Romance

Instead of opting for pastel colors and floral details, this wedding design invitation by **MARTA VELUDO** embraces geometric shapes and comes as a risographic print with fluorescent colors.

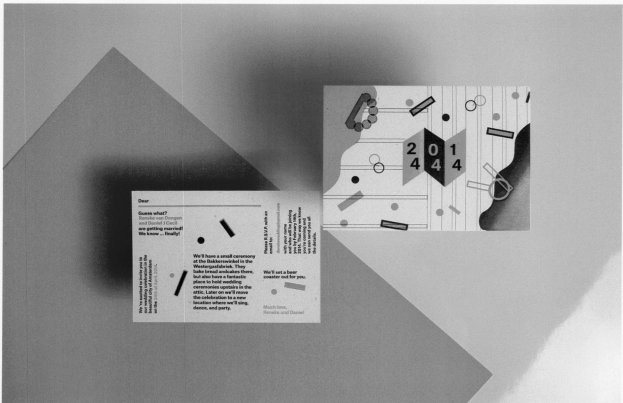

THE HEPWORTH
PRIZE FOR
SCULPTURE

•WE'RE
HAVING
A PARTY

...and we'd love you to join us!

Opening Party, 7–10pm
Thursday 20 October 2016
The Hepworth Wakefield

OPENING PARTY, 7–10PM
THURSDAY 20 OCTOBER 2016 —
Celebrate with us at the
opening of the UK's newest art
prize. Be the first to see our
largest exhibition ever, featuring
the work of shortlisted artists
*Phyllida Barlow, Steven
Claydon, Helen Marten* and
David Medalla.

**NO NEED TO RSVP,
JUST TURN UP!**

FREE — Aesop give-a-ways
throughout the evening.

Food & drink offers in our café bar.

HOW TO GET HERE — A regular
train service operates from Leeds
and Sheffield to Wakefield Kirkgate
and Wakefield Westgate stations,
approx. 5 and 15 minutes walk from
the gallery.

Free parking is available 5–10pm
in our car park, situated on Thornes
Lane, WF1 5QJ.

The Hepworth Wakefield
Gallery Walk, Wakefield WF1 5AW

HEPWORTHWAKEFIELD.ORG/PRIZE
#HepworthPrize

7—9

LIVE MUSIC
PERFORMANCES

7—10

RESIDENT DJ
ANDY HICKFORD

THE
HEPWORTH
WAKEFIELD

Supporting Sponsors:
Mtec
Litestructures

Media Partner:
Yorkshire Post

The Hepworth Wakefield is funded by Wakefield Council and Arts Council England. Registered charity 1131187.

---

mes Two

Designed by PASSPORT, two different invitations for the same
exhibition welcome one set of guests to an awards dinner and a
to an informal celebration on opening night.

PHYLLIDA
BARLOW/
STEVEN
CLAYDON/
HELEN
MARTEN/
DAVID
MEDALLA

21 October 2016 – 19 February 2017
hepworthwakefield.org/prize

THE HEPWORTH
PRIZE FOR
SCULPTURE

The Chair and Trustees invite you and a guest to
celebrate the opening of The Hepworth Prize for
Sculpture exhibition on Thursday 20 October.

6 – 7pm
Drinks reception & private view

6.30pm
Speeches

7 – 10pm
Public opening

This new £30,000 biennial award is open to artists
of any age and at any stage in their career, with
the shortlist based on the significance of their
contribution to sculpture in its broadest definition.

RSVP@hepworthwakefield.org
01924 247365
Please RSVP by Thursday 13 October

THE
HEPWORTH
WAKEFIELD

Supporting Sponsors:
Mtec
Litestructures

Media Partner:
Yorkshire Post

Asia Forbes and Mary Laura Krabill
boldhouse
6900 Camrose Drive
LOS ANGELES, CAL
9   0   0

Kindly *Reply* by July 15th

M _____

____ Attending   ____ Celebrating from afar

Please indicate entrée selection

____ Lawry's Prime Rib   ____ Mahi Mahi   ____ Vegetarian

and

Gail & Ian Jardin-
request the honor of your
at the marriage o

Jessica Jean Jo
to
Timothy Jordan

Saturday, the third of Se
two thousand and six
at five o'clock in the aft

The Los Angeles River Cent
570 West Avenue
Los Angeles, Californi

Dinner and dancing to
black tie optiona

Tropical Glam

Modern wedding invitations
from **BOLDHOUSE CREATIVE** marry a classic L.A.
locale with retro Hawaiian vibes.

Inspired by the old Hollywood glamour of the Beverly Hills Hotel in Los Angeles as well as a vintage Hawaiian aesthetic, Boldhouse Creative set out to design a wedding invitation suite that echoes these elements. The final invitations feature a combination of flat full-color printing and gold foil letterpress on duplexed cotton paper. Designer Asia Forbes provided the hand-lettering as a nod to the iconic Beverly Hills Hotel logo. Emerald letterpress and a bold striped liner serve to customize the metallic gold envelopes, which were addressed by hand using a modern calligraphy technique that mimics the typographic style showcased in the main piece. ❮

KINDLY
REPLY BY FEBRUARY 11TH 2017

M _____

WOULDN'T MISS IT! _____   WILL CELEBRATE FROM AFAR _____

FRIDAY NIGHT **WELCOME PARTY**, TOO? YOU KNOW IT! _____

DINNER RECEPTION MEAL PREFERENCE

BEEF _____   CHICKEN _____   VEGETARIAN _____

SEND TO:
COURTNEY + GEOFFREY
...LIFORNIA | 91226

Palm Springs Modern

BOLDHOUSE CREATIVE combines
vintage photos with contemporary type for a
desert destination wedding.

Created for a weekend-long wedding celebration in Palm Springs, California, this invitation by Boldhouse Creative takes its inspiration from vintage photographs of the area and combines them with a contemporary sensibility that reflects the couple's love for bold, modern design. Using matte flat full-color printing on duplexed paper, white foil letterpress, and bold sans serif typography, the suite features an embossed geometric monogram and custom pattern for the main invitation and envelopes. ‹

LET'S
DIVE
RIGHT
IN

WELCOME
POOL PARTY

HALF PAST SIX
FRIDAY NIGHT
DIVE-IN MOVIE
TACOS + MARGS

PRESIDIO POOL
AVALON HOTEL
PALM SPRINGS

BEFORE YOU GO, BRUNCH.

ELEVEN O'CLOCK
SUNDAY MORNING

TROPICALE RESTAURANT
330 EAST AMADO ROAD PALM SPRINGS, CALIFORNIA

C + G

ALONG WITH THEIR FAMILIES,

**COURTNEY DANIELLE LABREE
+ GEOFFREY EDWARD DOLEMAN**

INVITE YOU TO JOIN THEM IN CELEBRATING THEIR MARRIAGE

SATURDAY, THE EIGHTEENTH OF MARCH, TWO THOUSAND SEVENTEEN

AT HALF PAST FIVE O'CLOCK IN THE AFTERNOON

THE AVALON HOTEL

415 SOUTH BELARDO ROAD, PALM SPRINGS, CALIFORNIA

Postcards from Singapore

DREAM GIANT CREATIVE reimagines vintage postcards for a celebration in a historic city center.

Singapore's old town served as the jumping off point for this wedding invitation by Dream Giant Creative. Located on the Singapore River and framed by the modern buildings of the city's financial district, the venue's nostalgic flair was echoed in vintage-style postcard invitations. A modern art deco style illustration of the bride and groom in their wedding attire covers the front. On the reverse side, details are first handwritten, and then scanned and printed to achieve a handmade look. Each piece is hand-cut to recreate the scalloped edges found on vintage postcards. ❮

FANGTING & DON'S WEDDING CELEBRATION

Together with our families,
Zheng FangTing + Don Darwin Ferry
request the pleasure of your company
at the celebration of our Marriage

Sunday, 15 January 2017
Ceremony at 11:00 am
Kindly be seated by 10:45am

Followed by lunch + Tea Ceremony
from 12:00 pm

Empress at Asian Civilizations Museum
1 Empress Place, #01-03, Singapore 179555

Dress code - Smart casual
RSVP to FangTing 9696 9323 or Don 8382 5364

Parking: Basement car park of the New Parliament House (5 min walk),
Six Battery Road (4 min walk) & Fullerton Hotel/One Fullerton car park (3 min walk)
Taxi / Car pick-up & drop-off: The Arts House (1 min walk) / Fullerton Hotel (3 min walk)
MRT: Raffles Place, Exit H (5 min walk) **Location Map:** acm.org.sg/visit-us/plan-your-visit

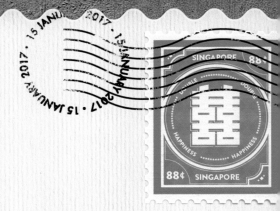

POST CARD

Address

Billy Zheng

246 Port Royal Avenue

Foster City Ca, 94404 USA

323A
Thomson
Road

307667
Singapore

— DON & FANGTING —

15 January 2017

OUR
BIG

Storybook Meeting

ESTHER POH's epic invitation to an annual gathering is anything but boring.

Annual meetings are rarely inspirational or interesting, and can even be a bit dull. But the members of the Design Studies Club at the Temasek School of Design knew that bold decision-making had the potential to bring about real change at their yearly get-together. Designer Esther Poh's concept for the event's invitation takes the form of a picture book. Weaving a story of exploration, it reflects the personality of the club's young members. The final illustrations by Ken Kaneko are encased in wood and reveal a Wes Anderson-inspired wonderland that encourages the recipient to venture into the proverbial woods and examine the year ahead from a different perspective. ❬

What started out with an invitation <u>Anna Bond</u> has
designed for her own wedding, has turned into a stationery empire
that now designs everything from notepads to shoes.

Rifle Paper Co.

Winter Park, Florida [USA]

When it became clear to designer and illustrator Anna Rifle Bond that she had a passion for stationery, she decided to print some cards and open an online store. That was in 2009. Since then, the small stationery line she started with her husband and business partner, Nathan Bond, has grown into a thriving business whose aesthetic and approach has changed the stationery market.

Before the couple first hit the publish button on riflepaperco.com, Bond was a freelance creative, who took on the project of designing her own wedding invitations. They were such a hit that she soon found herself designing invitations for family and friends. As clients began to share her work online, the response from the internet was greater and more immediate than anything she'd ever experienced, making her realize that she had something special on her hands. She was able to fund her first production of cards and products after several well-known blogs and magazines shared her work to an even broader audience—and the momentum has never stopped.

In addition to her right-on instincts and nuanced understanding of her customers and the market in general,

After being featured on blogs and in magazines, the first invitations Anna Bond and her partner, Nathan, sold funded the first production run of cards and products.

SAVE THE DATE

ALISON and CHRIS
are getting married
NOVEMBER 14, 2009
in PENINSULA, OHIO
invitation to follow

"I try to remain playful but not over the top in the composition, type elements, and color palette. It's easy to push too far, so I have to be critical, step back, and art direct my own work."

ANNA BOND

Bond's unique style is at the heart of Rifle Paper Co.'s success. Her immediately recognizable illustration style includes the hand-painted florals that dominate her work. As with everything she paints, she works in a style that is playful without being over the top in terms of composition and color palette.

Having organized events of all sizes, Bond's number one piece of advice when planning a wedding is not to stress and to enjoy the day for what it is: a gathering of loved ones. Beyond that, she points out that working within a budget, while essential, is easier than ever, now that beautiful stationery options are available at every price point.

A case in point is Rifle Paper Co.'s collaboration with digital stationery provider Paperless Post. Instead of looking at them as competitors, Bond saw an opportunity to create something new by harnessing the differences in their customer bases and areas of expertise. With each business sharing a passion for quality, customer care, and

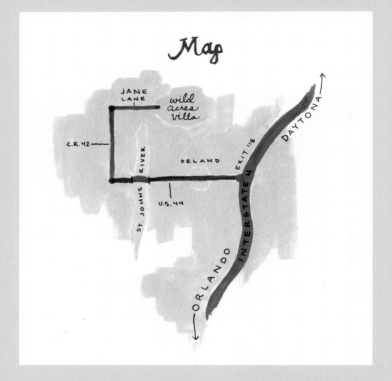

design, their collaboration has been a success, offering customers the option of digital stationery, and opening up even more pathways to beautiful communication.

In defining exactly what makes an outstanding invitation, Bond cites a unique invitation designed by a friend who worked at a letterpress company. The invitation was not only stunningly printed, but also had a vial of dried flowers and hand-lettering. With its balance between perfect presentation and personal touch, it is an example that seems to reflect the philosophy that Rifle Paper Co. has built its business on: the most personal moments in life are best shared with a handwritten card. ‹

The distinct illustration style and the attention to detail is what all of Rifle Paper Co.'s products have in common. It creates an unmistakingly personal and intimate touch, which has regained importance in the digital age.

WITH HEARTS FULL OF JOY
THE FAMILIES OF

Brittany Warren

& Bradley Conrad

INVITE YOU TO AN INTIMATE CELEBRATION
OF THEIR MARRIAGE ON
SATURDAY, THE TWENTY-SIXTH OF SEPTEMBER
TWO THOUSAND AND FIFTEEN
AT HALF PAST FOUR IN THE AFTERNOON
HÔTEL NELLIGAN
IN MONTRÉAL, QUÉBEC

———

Dinner and Dancing to Follow

The invitation sets the tone of the event. A well-crafted invitation package also contains beautiful menus, place cards, and other elements that underline the attention to detail.

Mike Vincenti
Readings by
n & Jared Miranda
ings
mberg
HE GLASS

1 Olive Street, No.
Brooklyn, NY
1

MANY
THANKS
from Sarah and Patrick

ROSEMARY AND MICHAEL BLUMBERG
INVITE YOU TO CELEBRATE WITH THEM AT
THE MARRIAGE OF THEIR DAUGHTER

Sarah Leigh Blumberg
TO
Patrick Keefe Whalen

SON OF NANCY & CORNELIUS WHALEN
SUNDAY THE 27TH OF JUNE, 2010
AT 6 O'CLOCK IN THE EVENING
The Park Restaurant
118 10TH AVENUE, NEW YORK, NY · RECEPTION TO FOLLOW
PATRICKANDSARAH.PROJECTWEDDING.COM

1 Olive Street, No.
Brooklyn, N.Y.
11211

R.S.V.P
BY MAY 19TH
We look forward to celebrating with you!

Name(s) _____

____ WILL BE THERE ____ NUMBER

____ UNABLE TO ATTEND

TOGETHER WITH THEIR FAMILIES

*Gabriela Esteves
and John La Rosa*

INVITE YOU TO CELEBRATE THEIR MARRIAGE
ON SATURDAY, THE TWENTY-FIFTH OF JANUARY
TWO THOUSAND FOURTEEN
AT TWO O'CLOCK IN THE AFTERNOON

CUVIER PARK
LA JOLLA, CALIFORNIA

Dinner & drinks to follow

CARMEN
PABLO

in honor of your company
celebration of their union
on the 10th of June 2017
o'clock in the afternoon

Hotel, 700 Third Avenue
le, Washington

and dancing to follow

After the ceremony, join us for an evening reception.
Cocktails and hors d'oeuvres at 5:00pm. Dinner will be served at 6:00pm,
dancing and merriment to follow.

Transportation will be provided to and from wedding ceremony and reception.
Shuttles will depart from the hotel lobby 45 minutes prior to each event
and return every half-hour, beginning at 9 pm.

RSVP

kindly reply until June 1st

__ can't wait

__ can't make it

send us this card in the mail at
8 Flower St., Seattle
or drop us a line at annaandjohn@us.

EN ♡ PABLO

save the date
10/06/2017

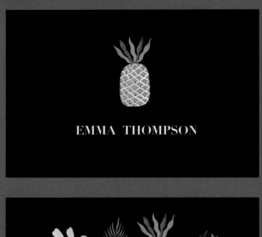

EMMA THOMPSON

CARMEN & PABLO

10 June 2017
Thank you for a wonderful day!

Folklore Fairytales

Romanian artist **MADALINA ANDRONIC** infuses her magical illustrations with the folklore of her homeland.

The Bucharest-based illustrator Madalina Andronic draws inspiration for her illustrated invitations from traditional Romanian fairytales and folklore. Her philosophy of incorporating thoughts of love and happiness into her designs while harnessing the magic of where she comes from helps to enrich the details and colors in her work. Radiating energy and love, Andronic's strong and distinctive style has served clients from around the world in various markets including publishing, editorial, advertising, and private commissions. ‹

ENTREE
House Mixed Lettuces,
Shallot and Thyme Vinaigrette,
Candied Pecans, Dried Cherries, Brie Cheese

MAIN
Nagano Pork Tenderloin
with Grainy Mustard Demi-Glace,
Served with Roasted Garlic Fork Mash
and Fresh Vegetables

DESSERT
Mascarpone Cheesecake with Lemon, Cherries,
Cocoa Nibs and Vanilla Bean Espuma

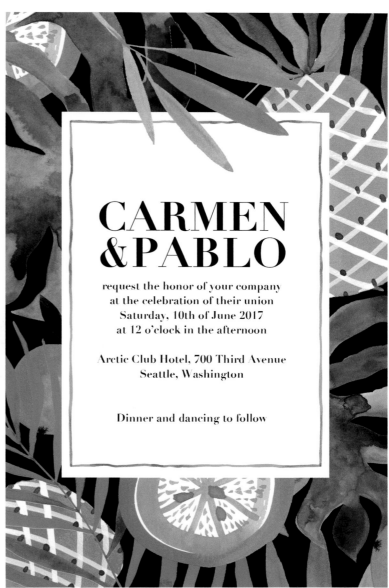

CARMEN &PABLO

request the honor of your company
at the celebration of their union
Saturday, 10th of June 2017
at 12 o'clock in the afternoon

Arctic Club Hotel, 700 Third Avenue
Seattle, Washington

Dinner and dancing to follow

Mimi & Albert

We request
the honor of your company
at the celebration of our union
Saturday, 10th of June 2017
at 12 o'clock in the afternoon

Arctic Club Hotel, 700 Third Avenue
Seattle, Washington

Dinner and dancing to follow

save the date
Mimi & Albert   **10 June 2017**

Emma Thompson

Mimi & Albert
10 June 2017

Thank you
for a wonderful day!

rsvp

kindly reply until June 1st
and let us know about your presence
and dietary requirements
send us this card in the mail at
8 Flower St., Seattle
or drop us a line at mimiandalbert@us.com

Starter

**House Mixed Lettuces, Shallot and Thyme Vinaigrette,
Candied Pecans, Dried Cherries, Brie Cheese**

Main

**Nagano Pork Tenderloin with Grainy Mustard Demi-Glace,
Served with Roasted Garlic Fork Mash and Fresh Vegetables**

Dessert

**Mascarpone Cheesecake with Lemon, Cherries,
Cocoa Nibs and Vanilla Bean Espuma**

ISABEL & JACK

ISABEL
SAVE TH

TOGETHER WITH OUR PARENTS,
WE REQUEST THE PLEASURE OF YOUR COMPANY
AT THE CELEBRATION OF THEIR UNION

JUNE 10, 2017
12:00 PM

ARCTIC CLUB HOTEL , 700 THIRD AVENUE
SEATTLE, WASHINGTON

DINNER AND DANCING TO FOLLOW

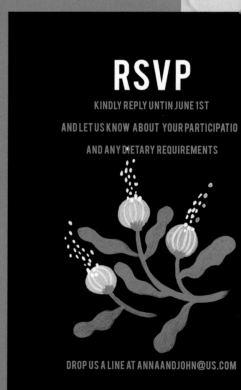

RSVP

KINDLY REPLY UNTIN JUNE 1ST
AND LET US KNOW ABOUT YOUR PARTICIPATIO
AND ANY DIETARY REQUIREMENTS

DROP US A LINE AT ANNAANDJOHN@US.COM

K
E
7

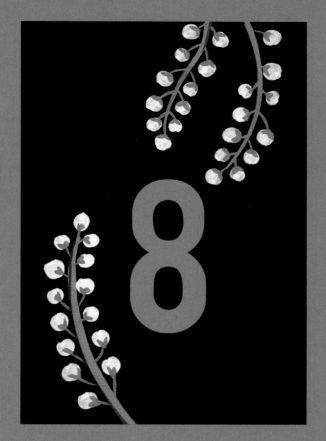

8

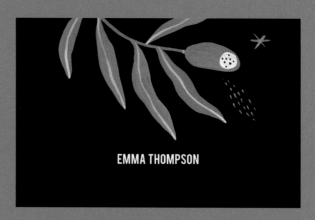

EMMA THOMPSON

ISABEL + JACK
10 JUNE 2017

THANK YOU FOR A WONDERFUL DAY!

STARTER
HOUSE MIXED LETTUCES, SHALLOT AND THYME VINAIGRETTE,
CANDIED PECANS, DRIED CHERRIES, BRIE CHEESE

MAIN
NAGANO PORK TENDERLOIN WITH GRAINY MUSTARD DEMI-GLACE,
SERVED WITH ROASTED GARLIC FORK MASH
AND FRESHMARKET VEGETABLES

DESSERT
MASCARPONE CHEESECAKE WITH LEMON,
CHERRIES, COCOA NIBS AND VANILLA BEAN ESPUMA

Poster Size

An oversized wedding invitation that doubles as a decorative poster by JACQUES & LISE commemorates a joyful and informal summer gathering of family and friends.

Nordic Birthday

Handmade with love and illustrated with ink and brush, **HELENA BERGENDAHL** created this invitation for a 50th birthday party.

Theo WIRD getauft!

DIE TAUFE UNSERES SOHNES
THEODOR PAUL
FINDET AM
SAMSTAG 20.09.2014 UM 14 UHR
IN DER THOMAS MORUS KIRCHE AM SCHAFBERG STATT.

BEI DIESER GELEGENHEIT WOLLEN WIR AUCH
UNSERE KIRCHLICHE TRAUUNG NACHHOLEN.

IM ANSCHLUSS WÜRDEN WIR UNS FREUEN,
WENN IHR MIT UNS IM
STEIRERSTÖCKL IN PÖTZLEINSDORF
FEIERT.

BARBARA ♥ CHRISTOPHER

Born in Pisces

Baptism invitations by ATELIER KARASINSKI take their
inspiration from 1950s illustrator Charley Harper.

Do It Yourself

Designer **IAN COLLINS** goes full DIY on the invitation for his wedding in the woods.

When Ian Collins and his future wife decided to get married in the woods, they also decided to design and produce their own wedding invitation. Printed on their home printer and laser cut with a rented cutter and engraver, the pop-up trees and overall look and feel of the invite provided their prospective guests with a taste of the event to come. The perforated RSVP card came with a detachable map of the surrounding area. An accordion-style field guide was also included with illustrations done by Collins's wife, which depict the local plants and animals. ❮

A Round Affair

Using her vintage letterpress machine, London-based illustrator and printmaker EMMA LEE CHENG creates coaster-like save the dates and invitations.

SAVE THE DATE

NAOMI & BEN
ARE GETTING MARRIED!

WEST YORKSHIRE
FORMAL INVITATION TO FOLLOW

03.09.2016

Save
the
Date

SAVE
THE DATE

ANTHONY & NICHOLAS ARE GETTING MARRIED · ANTHONY & NICHOLAS ARE GETTING MARRIED ·

16.1.16
LONDON

Before it was replaced by other methods, letterpress was the only means of printing.

"Traditionally, perfect letterpress printing would have been made using as little pressure as possible to create a totally flat impression. Nowadays a debossing effect is in high demand." Emma Lee Cheng

ANNA HALES & TOM SINGER

ohmigosh!

we're really doing it!

S I N G E R W E D D I N G

- -

we would love you to be there!

RSVP:
www.halesandsinger.com

12TH APRIL 2014

"We had a lot of information we wanted to get out to our guests and we didn't want to bombard them with a bunch of tiny pieces of paper, so we came up with a cheap solution to get some fun newsprints done."

NICK FRANCHI

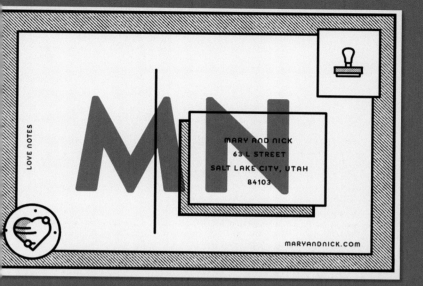

Off the Beaten Path

Graphic designer NICK FRANCHI sets out to put a unique spin on his own wedding invitations.

When designer Nick Franchi created the wedding invitations for his own wedding, he found the process substantially more difficult than working with a client. He and his fiancée knew that rather than the standard script-wielding invites, they wanted something unique—an invite that expressed both of their personalities and their desire to lead an adventurous life together. The final invitation suite included a save the date card, an invitation, an RSVP, coasters, a newspaper with the wedding details, and coordinating stickers. ❮

SUNNY
72°

VOLUME V.01

VOLUME V.01

MARY ◯ NICK

MARY AND NICK ARE GETTING MARRIED
MARYANDNICK.COM

M N

AUGUST 19, 2016

AUGUST 19, 2016

MARY & NICK ARE GETTING MARRIED! READ ALL ABOUT IT!

WE'D BE HONORED IF YOU WOULD JOIN US ON OUR SPECIAL DAY TO CELEBRATE OUR LOVE! AS THE PARTY GETS CLOSER WE WILL KEY YOU IN ON THE DETAILS AND PROVIDE YOU WITH HELPFUL INFORMATION. CHECK OUT OUR WEBSITE FOR UPDATES.

WE'D BE HONORED IF YOU WOULD JOIN US ON OUR SPECIAL DAY TO CELEBRATE OUR LOVE! AS THE PARTY GETS CLOSER WE WILL KEY YOU IN ON THE DETAILS AND PROVIDE YOU WITH HELPFUL INFORMATION. CHECK OUT OUR WEBSITE FOR UPDATES.

WE'D BE HONORED IF YOU WOULD JOIN US ON OUR SPECIAL DAY TO CELEBRATE OUR LOVE! AS THE PARTY GETS CLOSER WE WILL KEY YOU IN ON THE DETAILS AND PROVIDE YOU WITH HELPFUL INFORMATION. CHECK OUT OUR WEBSITE FOR UPDATES.

WE'D BE HONORED IF YOU WOULD JOIN US ON OUR SPECIAL DAY TO CELEBRATE OUR LOVE! AS THE PARTY GETS CLOSER WE WILL KEY YOU IN ON THE DETAILS AND PROVIDE YOU WITH HELPFUL INFORMATION. CHECK OUT OUR WEBSITE FOR UPDATES.

THE WEDDING LOCATION

BEAR MOUNTAIN INN & OVERLOOK LODGE
3020 SEVEN LAKES DRIVE BEAR MOUNTAIN
NEW YORK, 10911

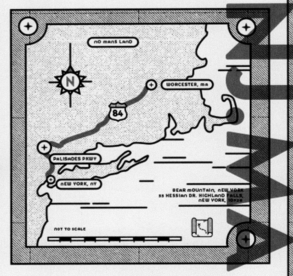

NO MANS LAND

N

WORCESTER, MA

84

PALISADES PKWY

NEW YORK, NY

BEAR MOUNTAIN, NEW YORK
55 HESSIAN DR. HIGHLAND FALLS,
NEW YORK, 10928

NOT TO SCALE

THE WEDDING PARTY

KERRI DEMICO

CAROL HENNESSEY KELLY

KERRI DEMICO

JOE FRANCHI

KEVIN RAPF

AUSTIN RICE

FROM NEW YORK CITY: TAKE GEORGE WASHINGTON BRIDGE UPPER DECK TO THE PALISADES INTERSTATE PARKWAY HEADING NORTH. TAKE THE PIP TO THE END (PAST EXIT 19). FOLLOW SIGNS TO 9W SOUTH FROM THE BEAR MOUNTAIN TRAFFIC CIRCLE

FROM WESTCHESTER AND CONNECTICUT: TAKE I-95 TO ROUTE 287. GO OVER THE TAPPAN ZEE BRIDGE. TAKE EXIT 13N ONTO THE PALISADES INTERSTATE PARKWAY (PIP) HEADING NORTH. TAKE THE PIP TO THE END (PAST EXIT 19). FOLLOW SIGNS TO 9W SOUTH FROM THE BEAR MOUNTAIN TRAFFIC CIRCLE..

DETAILS

CEREMONY
OVERLOOK LODGE AT BEAR MOUNTAIN

THE CEREMONY WILL TAKE PLACE OUTSIDE AT THE OVERLOOK LODGE AT BEAR MOUNTAIN. THIS PICTURE PERFECT SETTING OVERLOOKS THE BEAUTIFUL HUDSON RIVER JUST BELOW. INCASE OF RAIN THE CEREMONY WILL BE HELD INSIDE JUST STEPS AWAY FROM THE OUTSIDE DECK.

6:30 PM

RECEPTION
OVERLOOK LODGE AT BEAR MOUNTAIN

7:30 PM

THE MENU

DUO OF BEEF
PAN ROASTED FILET MIGNON, BRAISED BEEF SHORTRIB, CREAMY POLENTA, APPLE GLAZED CARROTS, SHORTRIB JUS
BEEF

FRENCH CHICKEN BREAST
TRUFFLED DAUPHINE POTATOES, SEASONAL VEGETABLES, NATURAL JUS
CHICKEN

ROASTED VEGETABLE LASAGNA
BASIL PESTO, BECHAMEL, SHAVED PECORINO
VEG

RSVP
WWW.MARYANDNICK.COM
OR MAIL IN RSVP CARD INCLUDED

LODGING

OVERLOOK LODGE

WE HOPE THAT YOU NOT ONLY COME TO THE PARTY BUT CHOOSE TO SPEND THE NIGHT! THEOVERLOOK LODGE OFFERS 24 ROOMS WITH EITHER 1 KING BED OR 2 DOUBLE BEDS. JOIN US FORBREAKFAST THE NEXT DAY AND TAKE ADVANTAGE OF THE HIKING AND SWIMMING IN THE PARKDURING THE BEAUTIFUL SUMMER! THE BEAR MOUNTAIN INN HAS GREAT DINING AND A SPA TO OFFERAS WELL! CHECK OUT THE BEAR MOUNTAIN'S WEBSITE FOR BOOKING. IF YOU WANT TO STAY WITH USAT THE OVERLOOK LODGE - BE SURE TO BOOK IT BEFORE JULY 5TH TO ENSURE YOUR RESERVATION.

WWW.VISITBEARMOUNTAIN.COM/OVER-LOOK-LODGE.HTM

845.786.2731

WORD SEARCH

```
V  N  E  W  J  E  R  S  E  V  Q  S
M  C  I  E  F  L  O  W  E  R  N  T
M  E  S  F  K  J  V  D  Z  O  C  M
G  M  A  I  U  A  S  F  W  M  E  O
N  E  O  T  L  T  L  B  V  A  C  U
I  S  U  O  B  L  O  T  G  R  A  N
K  R  H  A  R  A  V  J  L  V  P  T
O  A  C  H  R  E  L  Z  E  A  S  A
O  T  K  D  O  J  T  L  W  Z  S  I
C  S  I  N  D  H  J  A  S  S  A  N
J  N  D  A  L  A  S  A  T  S  A  P
G  G  N  I  I  K  S  R  N  S  S  B
```

ALTERNATE LODGING

THE THAYER HOTEL

THIS LANDMARK HOTEL, ON THE GROUNDS OF THE U.S. MILITARY ACADEMY, OVERLOOKS HUDSON RIVER. IT'S A 0.4-MILE WALK FROM THE WEST POINT MUSEUM

6.7 MILES AWAY.

HOLIDAY INN

WELL IT'S A HOLIDAY INN WHAT ELSE CAN WE SAY. ACTUALLY WE CAN SAY THAT IT WAS RATED 4.5 STARS OUT OF 5.

4 MILES AWAY

SO MANY THINGS TO DO AT BEAR MOUNTAIN

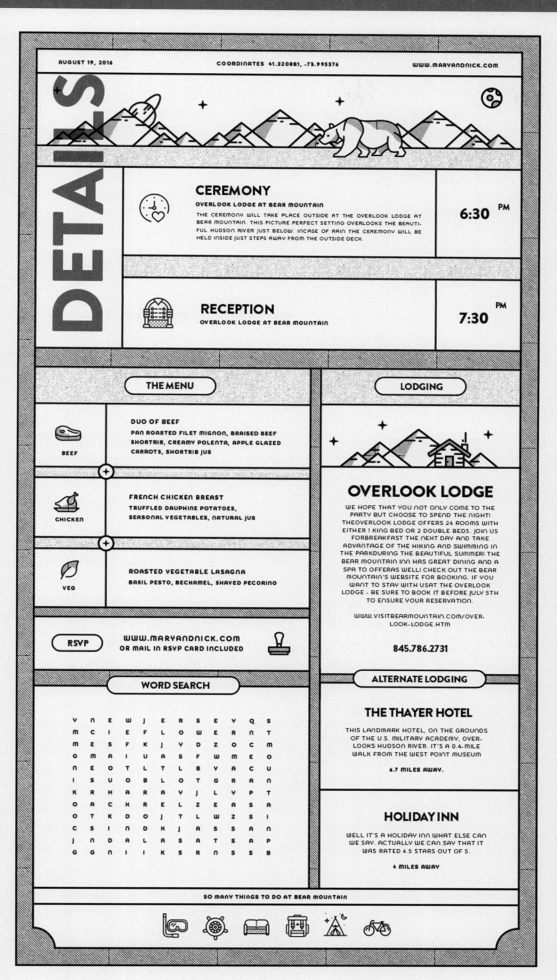

Good Enough to Eat

OLLANSKI's invitation to a Kangaroos Deutschland event looks suspiciously like a hamburger on a sesame seed bun.

Outside the Norm

JANAR SINILOO and ANDERS BAKKEN's invitation for the 2015 Estonian Art Directors Club Design Awards opens into a poster, with the folded areas separating information into easy-to-read text boxes.

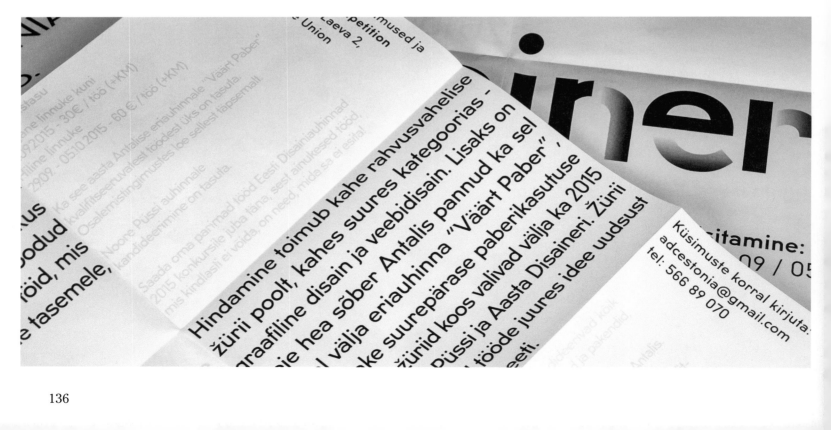

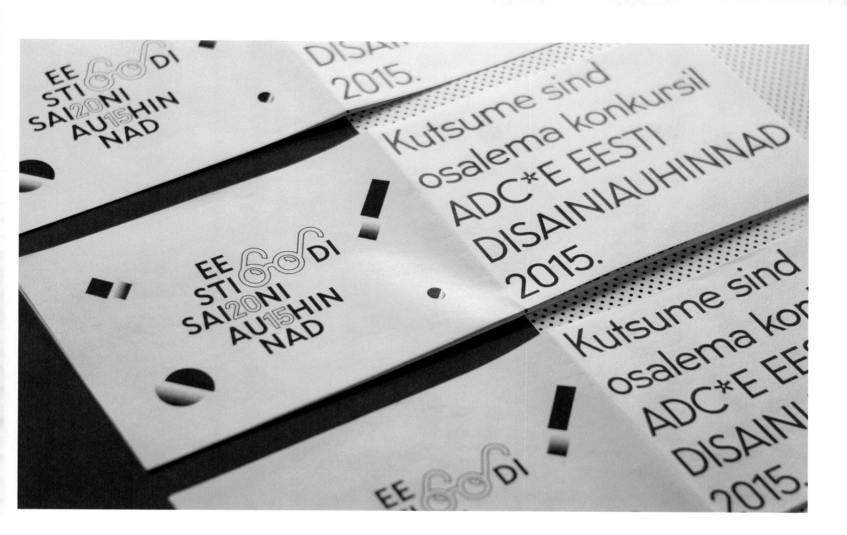

Two in One

LUMINOUS DESIGN GROUP creates
an oversized invitation for two special events
held on the same day.

Created for a simultaneous wedding and christening celebration, this invitation needed to communicate a number of things at once. Luminous Design Group found a clever solution for the unusual event in a poster-size invitation. Written on one side are details of the day's events, while the other side uses infographics to tell the family's story. Because three people were at the center of the day, the triangle became a repeated design element in both the shape of the box holding the poster and the event logo, which incorporates the participants' initials. Printed on kraft paper with black ink, the style reflects the industrial space where the occasion took place. ❮

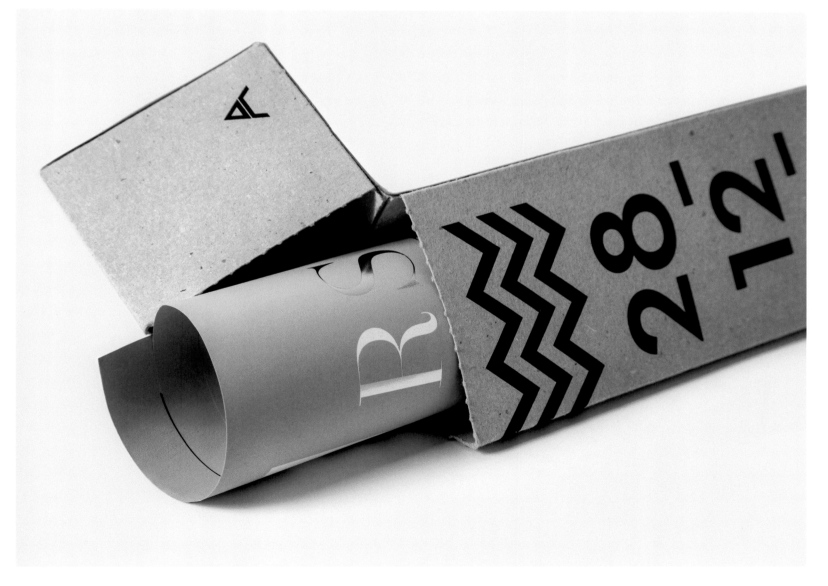

139

M is for Marriage

A South Asian wedding invitation by **MUSTAALI RAJ** strikes the perfect balance between old and new.

Designer Mustaali Raj's approach to the wedding invitations for Mustaali and Minahil's traditional South Asian wedding held in Vancouver, BC, brings an artfully contemporary flair to the event. Soft colors and gold foil paired with geometric layouts bridge the traditions, cultures, and places that define the day's celebrations. The couple's logo is derived from the letter M in both Hindi (representing Mustaali's Indian heritage) and Urdu (representing Minahil's Pakistani heritage). ❮

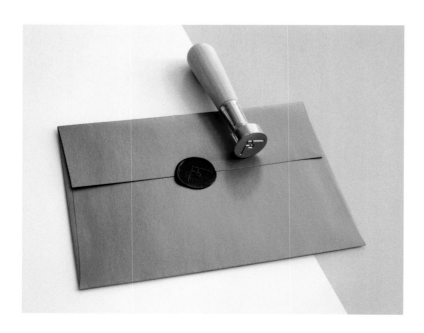

In the name of Allah, the most Gracious, the most Merciful

Mustansir & Sakina Baq kindly request your presence at the Waleema ceremony of their beloved son

MUSTAALI with MINA...

daughter of Mr. & Mrs. A...

May 0...
Sa...

MA – LETTER M IN HINDI

WALIMA

BARAT

Tiny House

BOLD STOCKHOLM's invitation to a home collection
debut cleverly folds into a miniature room.

In 2009, Swedish fashion retailer H&M successfully expanded
into the home furnishings market. For their 2012 collection,
creative agency Studio Noc built an oversized dollhouse featuring different parts of the collection in each of its rooms. Bold
Stockholm created a concept and design for the event's invitation featuring a folded card that transforms into a room, with
patterns from the new collection decorating the walls. The give-
aways at the event were mostly copper-colored, so the designer
printed all text with copper foil on sandy beige paper. All units
have a minimalistic exterior and full-color patterned interiors. ❮

DKNY
FALL 2016 COLLECTION

SECTION _____ ROW
RSVP.FASHIONGPS.COM/DKNY

FALL 2016 COLLECTION

Billboard-Inspired

COMMISSION STUDIO's hands-on
production process produces one-of-a-kind
invitations for a fashion show.

The invitations and press packs designed by Commission Studio for the DKNY Fall 2016 presentation, held at Skylight Modern in New York, were inspired by the collage pattern of torn billboards and rose motifs found on the silks and leathers in the collection; the invitations became a physical interpretation of the pattern. Printed in a run of 750 copies, they were then layered, bound, and torn by hand in-house so that every invitation was completely unique. The materials not only reflected the signature print, but also the raw space in which the presentation took place. Press packs that greeted guests on arrival were individually torn in the same format as the invitations. ‹

Time and Being

To highlight this couple's passion for fine art and their preference for a modern aesthetic, **YONDER DESIGN** created a suite featuring black leather, gray paper, and a marbled envelope liner with gold accents.

YES / NO

LIST NAMES · DIETARY RESTRICTIONS · ARRIVAL DATE

WWW.CHRIS-JOHN.COM

REPLY BEFORE
11/1
TWO THOUSAND SIXTEEN

LEWISTON, MAINE
C | J
THOUSAND SIXTEEN

THEATER SEAT

WELCOME
PARTY

FAREWELL
BRUNCH

YOUR PRESENCE IS REQUESTED
AT THE MARRIAGE OF

CHRIS | JOHN

THURSDAY : THE FIRST OF DECEMBER
TWO THOUSAND SIXTEEN
HALF PAST FIVE IN THE AFTERNOON

THE OLD MILL
LEWISTON · MAINE

FORMAL ATTIRE

CHRIS

ROASTED
CANDIED

THE FAVOR OF YOUR REPLY
IS REQUESTED BY
the twenty-third of February

M_____
_____ *Number attending*

_____ ACCEPTS WITH PLEASURE
_____ DECLINES WITH REGRET

U.S.
47

Accommodations

The Ritz-Carlton Dallas
2121 MCKINNEY AVENUE
DALLAS, TEXAS

The Adolphus Hotel
1321 COMMERCE STREET
DALLAS, TEXAS

Please visit our wedding website below for
details & information regarding hotel room accommodations:
WWW.JEANIELOVESRICH.COM

Modern Fairytale

A little bit of sparkle transforms these wedding invitations by CECI NEW YORK into something magical.

Inspired by the client's desire to do things differently, designer Ceci Johnson and her team created a complex, hexagonal origami wedding invitation for the event. The design, which embodies a magical fairytale, uses rose gold and a bit of sparkle to achieve the perfect mood. Assembling the final 150 invitations required the designers to hand-fold each individual piece. In addition to the invitations, Ceci New York designed all of the day's accessories. The special attention paid to branding the event, which took place at the Dallas Arboretum and the Ritz Carlton, tied the day's celebrations together. ❮

149

Ashley AND
Mike
1945 WASHINGTON ST. #504
SAN FRANCISCO, CA 94109

SAVE THE DATE
Ashley AND
Mike
OCTOBER 3, 2015

CARMEL ← CALIFORNIA
ASHLEYANDMIKE2015.COM

A & M

BEFORE THEY MEE
IN THE REDWOODS TO SA
PLEASE JOIN US FOR
REHEARSAL DINNER CELEB

Ashley and

THURSDAY, OCTOBER
COCKTAILS AT 6 PM & DINI
THE CLUBHOUSE AT SANTA LU
CARMEL, CALIFORNI

HOSTED BY MR. & MRS. MICH

TRANSPORTATION WILL BE PR
GUESTS NOT STAYING AT SANTA L

RSVP TO SUZYQ3179 @AC

Ashley & Mike
FOR MORE DETAILS
ASHLEYANDMIKE2015.COM

WITH GREAT JOY
MR. & MRS CHARLES FISCHER
INVITE YOU TO CELEBRATE THE MARRIAGE OF

Ashley Marie
AND
Michael Edward Stern Jr.

SATURDAY, THE THIRD OF OCTOBER
AT FOUR O'CLOCK IN THE AFTERNOON
SANTA LUCIA PRESERVE
CARMEL, CALIFORNIA

MERRIMENT TO FOLLOW

Dance by the light of the moon

We Met at a Bar

The inspiration for this playful invitation designed by **SHIPWRIGHT & CO.** comes straight from the couple's dating history.

Ashley and Mike had many dates at New York's atmospheric Bemelmans Bar, nestled inside the historic Carlyle Hotel. Named after Ludwig Bemelmans, the creator of the *Madeline* books, its walls are covered with his illustrations of animals frolicking in the woods. These scenes inspired the couple to ask for similar imagery in their wedding invitations. The save the dates capture the animals dancing at dusk on the barn where Ashley and Mike tied the knot, while the invitations move into a nighttime world layered in three colors, with handwritten text filling up the full moon. Every piece's beauty is in the details, with each animal and plant specifically chosen for the place they sit. ❮

BASTERÀ UN PIZZICO
PER FARTI GRATTARE,
CON MILLE STARNUTI
TI FARÀ DIMENARE

Adventures in Matrimony

MONDO·MOMBO finds inspiration for wedding stationery in a classic game.

Do not begin unless you intend to finish. The first rule of the game Jumanji struck the designers at Mondo·Mombo as ironically relevant to the adventure of marriage, inspiring them to design wedding stationery based on the game. The playful result arrives in a wooden box engraved with the couple's names, and contains a pair of dice that reference a quote from the Jumanji movie. Other quotes can be found in the smallest details on the menus as well as in a branded guestbook. Enclosed with the invitation and RSVP are a pawn and two dice that invite guests to accompany the bride and groom on their new adventure. ❮

CHE SIA D'ORO

O DI DIAMANTE

SIA PREZIOSO

O A BUON MERCATO,

SE CI PASSA

UNA FALANGE

IL TUO CUOR SARÀ

AFFERRATO

BASTERÀ UN PIZZICO

PER FARTI GRATTARE,

CON MILLE STARNUTI

TI FARÀ DIMENARE

All About Letterpress

SHIPWRIGHT & CO.'s custom-designed letterpress invite reflects their client's style, love story, and sense of humor.

A simple and personal suite for Emily and Jim illustrates the grandeur of Yosemite, where their winter wedding celebration took place. Shipwright & Co. created three layers of custom-illustrated pieces with two die-cut layers depicting the park's mountainous landscape. When removed, the layers reveal the main invitation highlighting details of the event. The designers combined line drawing with elegant hand-lettering, striking a balance between campy and classy by keeping things a bit quirky. Each piece is printed in gray, green, blue, and white inks. Smoky gray and soft blue paper, as well as deep blue and green envelopes, create a serene winter color palette. ❮

Emily & Jim
6316 17th Ave NW
Seattle, WA 98107

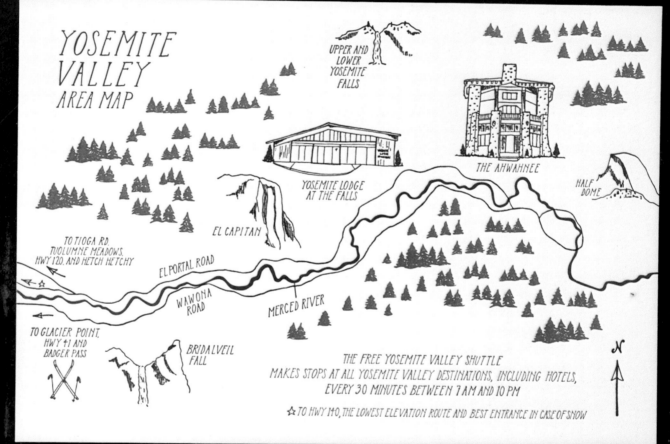

YOSEMITE
VALLEY
AREA MAP

UPPER AND LOWER YOSEMITE FALLS

THE AHWAHNEE

HALF DOME

YOSEMITE LODGE AT THE FALLS

EL CAPITAN

TO TIOGA RD, TUOLUMNE MEADOWS, HWY 120, AND HETCH HETCHY

EL PORTAL ROAD

WAWONA ROAD

MERCED RIVER

TO GLACIER POINT, HWY 41 AND BADGER PASS

BRIDALVEIL FALL

THE FREE YOSEMITE VALLEY SHUTTLE
MAKES STOPS AT ALL YOSEMITE VALLEY DESTINATIONS, INCLUDING HOTELS,
EVERY 30 MINUTES BETWEEN 7 AM AND 10 PM

☆ TO HWY 140, THE LOWEST ELEVATION ROUTE AND BEST ENTRANCE IN CASE OF SNOW

N

OF NATURE

N YOSEMITE?

ELY!
MARRIED IN JUNE
S OUT.)

TRÉE SELECTION

Oryza

TRICTIONS?

Rich Symbolism

An illustrated wedding invitation by MONDO·MOMBO weaves together textured symbols to tell a couple's story.

ISTRUZIONI

1. ASSICURATI CHE LA PELLE SIA · PULITA
2. RIMUOVI LA PELLICOLA PROTETTIVA E FAI ADERIRE IL TATUAGGIO ALLA · PELLE BEN · ASCIUTTA CON UNA · LEGGERA PRESSIONE
3. BAGNA IL RETRO DEL TATUAGGIO CON UNA SPUGNETTA PER · CIRCA 30 SECONDI
4. SOLLEVA IL SUPPORTO DI · CARTA CON DELICATEZZA

TAG THE DAY

Ilaria E Emanuele

2 · GIUGNO 2 · 0 · 1 · 6

let's drink AND dance!

THE WEDDING PARTY
02 · 06 · 2016
ORE · VENTITRE
Villa la Garomba
MONCHIERO

ILARIAEMANUELE

The attention to detail and the haptic experience of
their work have made Studio on Fire a reference for an effective blend of
modern designs and vintage production methods.

Studio on Fire

Saint Paul, Minnesota [USA]

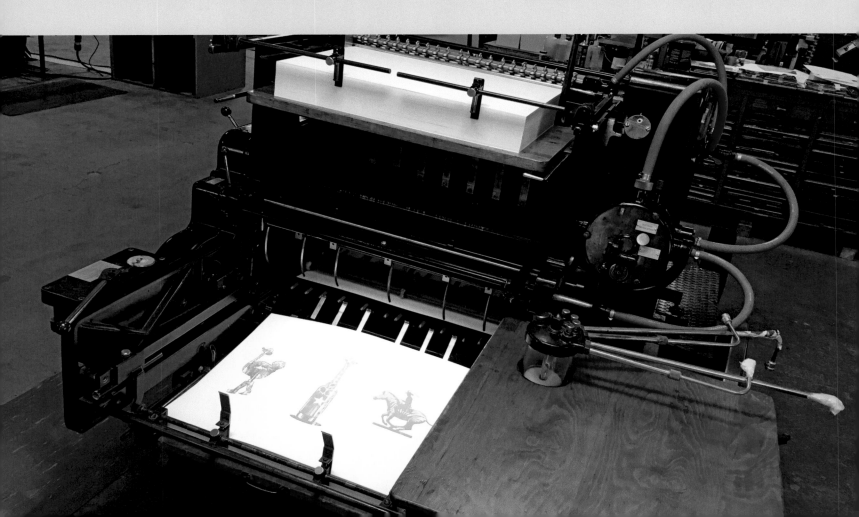

Studio on Fire's first press was located in founder Ben Levitz's basement, nestled between the water heater and the cat's litter box. At that time, Levitz worked days in the advertising industry and long nights at home on his side gig. It is interesting to note that he considered studying sculpture in college; his little basement printing studio would go on to make a name for itself creating beautiful printed objects, guided by a philosophy that clearly echoes a fine art approach to materials and concepts.

Twenty years after those late nights at home, Studio on Fire operates out of a warehouse space in Saint Paul,

Minnesota, and employs 15 people whose diverse creative backgrounds play a major role in its innovative spirit. The collective abilities of the studio's employees, which include everything from painting and photography to pottery and furniture-making, inform its creative sensibilities and ensure a fierce attention to detail.

With such a flexible and talented team, Studio on Fire is well prepared to push the boundaries of modern letterpress, creating unforgettable printed pieces that recipients are happy to display in their homes. Using modern technology to actualize the quality, artisan characteristics that make each product feel unique and handmade, they

trade wood and metal type for a process that translates digital files into photopolymer plates. Over the years, they have added a number of additional specialties to their roster, including foil and engraving that pair with letterpress to create endless options for customization.

When working with such a wide range of techniques, it is invaluable to have an experienced designer who can guide the process and make informed decisions that fit the concept behind each invitation. When it comes to making design and printing decisions, the studio's designers operate under the firm belief that there is a difference between what can be done and what should be done. Senior designer Sam Michaels also points out that the design process is usually driven by the client's choice of materials or processes. A request for foil stamping, for example, opens

Above: For these custom designed and letterpress printed wedding suite a hand-drawn map was used across several elements while elegant typography and a limited two-ink color palette kept things classy.

the door to printing on colored stock, whereas letterpress printing allows the designers to play with the transparent quality of the inks and create additional colors with overprinting. Rather than flash and gimmick, simple and clever solutions are the focus of their work. They have learned that the temptation to get too elaborate with specialty processes like die and laser cutting can lead to invitations that don't have any reasoning behind their aesthetic choices.

What ultimately defines a well-crafted invitation for Studio on Fire? Something that knocks the recipient's socks off, makes them feel special when receiving it, and gets them excited to attend the event. But perhaps the highest achievement is crafting an invitation that has the power to make the recipient feel bad about throwing it away. ‹

Page 162: Some of the letterpress machines in the studio stem from the 1950s and 1960s. Using these vintage presses with modern letterpress techniques adds a crisp and vibrant touch to Studio on Fire's work.

"We think about craft like riding a bike—it is just second nature."

The studio's designers operate under the firm belief that there is a difference between what could be done and what should be done when it comes to making design and printing decisions.

ACCOMMODATIONS

PLEASE
RSVP
BEFORE
APRIL

DAVID AND MONICA NASSIF INVITE YOU
TO CELEBRATE THE MARRIAGE OF

Calla
NASSIF
AND
Jayme
MURPHY

FAME LAUNDRY HOUSE
60 SOUTH 6TH STREET, SUITE 2600
MINNEAPOLIS, MN 55402

TAME YOUR MUSTACHES

GENTLEMEN

PASSWORD NO PARTY

FAME LAUNDRY HOUSE

THERE'S NOTHING DRY ABOUT OUR CLEANING, SO WASH AWA

WITH OUR IRRESISTIBLY STRONG SOLVENTS AND DECADENT D

AND IF YOU'RE NOT GAME FOR A RAUCOUS GET-TOGETHER, I

YOUR REPUTATION MAY NOT BE SOILED ENOUGH FOR OUR I

OF COURSE, WE CAN HELP WITH THAT.

For its annual open house event, Fame Retail made it a tradition to build the theme around the selection of food and drinks they would serve. In 2012, with a nod to 1920s prohibition, they came up with the idea for speakeasy-inspired invitations. The white cards were letterpress-printed while silver ink and a tonal letterpress varnish were used on the black cards.

… Mustachioed gents, pin-curled ladies, icons of delicate line-work, and plenty of liquor lingo.

APRIL 26TH 201

60 SOUTH 6TH STREET, SUITE 2600 MINN

LOOK FOR THE SIGN THAT SAYS FAME LAUN

FROM FIVE O'CLOCK UNTIL THE COPS RAID

GET SNOCKERED & STUF

WE'LL BE SERVING SIGNATURE COCKTAILS AND SAV

JUST LIKE YOUR GREAT GRANDMA USED TO MAKE. IF SHE W

CLEAN UP, OR GET CLEANED

IT'S REALLY UP TO THE CARDS, ISN'T IT? BRING LADY LU

PLUS ONE, & TRY YOUR HAND AT ONE OF

ME LIPSTICK

GENTLEMEN

TAME YOUR MUSTACHES

FOLLOW GOODTIME CHARLIE

HE POURS A MEAN DRINK. AND DISPENSES SOMEWHAT USELESS ADVICE.
FOLLOW GOODTIME CHARLIE'S RANDOM MUSINGS ON TWITTER AT
TWITTER.COM/FAMESPEAKEASY

Purveyors of Pork

For the Friends of Ham store opening in Ilkley, England, PASSPORT designed a promotional invitation that seamlessly partners with the shop's other print collateral.

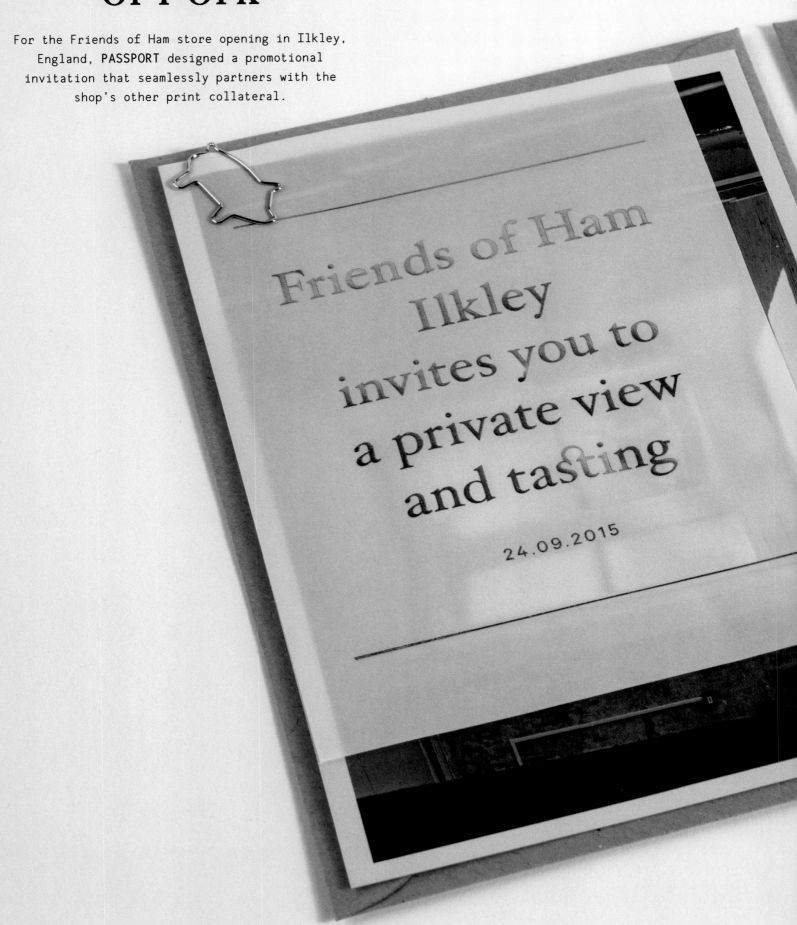

Friends of Ham
Ilkley
invites you to
a private view
and tasting

24.09.2015

FRIENDS OF HAM

Join us for an exclusive evening to celebrate the newly
opened Friends of Ham in Ilkley. We'll be offering an
array of mouth-watering meats, cheeses and charcuterie,
accompanied by our extensive menu of beers, wines and
spirits, alongside freshly baked goodies and great coffee.

Doors will open at **7pm on Thursday 24th September**

Please **RSVP to: lucy@lucyallenpr.co.uk**

...ng this invitation at the bar for your **free** welcome

...t – Trot On!

Address	Friends of Ham
	8 Wells Road
	Ilkley
	LS29 9JD
Social	Instagram: framilkley
	Twitter: @fohilkley
	facebook.com/friendsofhamilkley

SAVE THE DATE

N HOPE FRIE
TLES BURNS B

married on Septem

ORK   INVITAT

HOPEAN...

WEDDING DETAILS
September 10, 2016
Tarrytown, New York

KINDLY REPLY
by August 10th

NAME(S)

ACCEPTS ....   REGRETS ....

MR. AND MRS. JEFFREY OWEN FRIEDLAND
REQUEST THE PLEASURE OF YOUR COMPANY
AT THE MARRIAGE OF THEIR DAUGHTER

Lauren Hope Friedland

TO

Miles Burns Begin

SATURDAY, THE TENTH OF SEPTEMBER
AT HALF PAST SIX
BLUE HILL AT STONE BARNS
TARRYTOWN, NEW YORK

NER AND DANCING TO FO...
BLACK TIE OPTIONAL

Farm to Table

An elaborate wedding invitation suite by ROBINSON PRESS brings a custom celebration to life.

For their farm-to-table wedding celebration at Blue Hill at Stone Barns restaurant, Hope and Miles sent out save the date cards inspired by antique seed packet designs. In keeping with the rustically floral theme, the invitations mix antique botanical illustrations with artful borders, and are enclosed in hand-lettered envelopes by Leveret & Hare. Robinson Press added copper foil details and enlarged a lavender illustration to create an abstract foil-pressed envelope liner. Letterpress printed on Reich Savoy double thick cotton paper, each piece has a special personality that reflects the spirit of the day. ‹

HOPE & MILES

SEPTEMBER 10, 2016
Blue Hill at Stone Barns
TARRYTOWN, NEW YORK

MR. AND MRS. JEFFREY OWEN FRIEDLAND
REQUEST THE PLEASURE OF YOUR COMPANY
AT THE MARRIAGE OF THEIR DAUGHTER

Lauren Hope Friedland

WEDDING DETAILS

September 10, 2016
Tarrytown, New York

...SPORTATION WILL BE PROVIDE...
... FROM THE WEDDING AND T...

...OMMODATE THEM AT...
...MONY AND RECEPTION.

...WEBSITE FOR MOR...
...OUT TRAVEL...
...IONS...

SAVE THE DATE

LAUREN HOPE FRIEDLAND & MILES BURNS BEGIN

are getting married on September 10, 2016

TARRYTOWN, NEW YORK

INVITATION TO FOLLOW

HOPEANDMILES.COM
PASSWORD: FARMTOTABLE

...AY, THE TENTH OF SEPTEMBER
AT HALF PAST SIX
BLUE HILL AT STONE BARNS
TARRYTOWN, NEW YORK

DINNER AND DANCING TO FOLLOW
BLACK TIE OPTIONAL

ACCEPTS _____ NAME(S) _____

REGRETS _____

SAVE THE DATE

LAUREN HOPE FRIEDLAND
& MILES BURNS BEGIN

are getting married on September 10, 2016

TARRYTOWN, NEW YORK

HOPEANDMILES.COM
PASSWORD: FARMTOTABLE

INVITATION TO FOLLOW

Mr. and Mrs. Jeffrey Owen F...

SEVEN POLO FIELD LANE

WEDDING DETAILS
September 10, 2016
Tarrytown, New York

TRANS...
T...

HOPE & MILES
WEDDING WEEKEND

HOPE & MILES

SEPTEMBER 10, 2016
Blue Hill at Stone Barns
TARRYTOWN, NEW YORK

...HILDREN, BUT UNFORTUNATELY
...ATE THEM AT THE
...NG CEREMONY AND RECEPTION.

...WEDDING WEBSITE FOR MORE
...ATION ABOUT TRAVEL AND
...CCOMMODATIONS.

...ANDMILES.COM
...D: FARMTOTABLE

LOVE
IS ALL YOU NEED

FANNY ET PASCAL

VOUS ACCUEILLERONS
POUR UN DÎNER QUI SERA SERVI
AU CHÂTEAU PARADIS À PARTIR DE 20H .

DÎNER

ET PASCAL

'OUS FAIRE PART DE LEUR
AURA LIEU LE SAMEDI

5.2017

ÉRÉMONIE, LES FAMILLES
IR DE VOUS ACCUEILLIR
AIL AU CAFÉ DE PARIS À
À PARTIR DE 18H30.

TIMBRE

RSVP

Pretty in Pink

Bride and Groom Fanny and Pascal
requested that the RUBAN COLLECTIF design
a modern wedding invitation with an array
of pinks printed on textured paper.

LOV

IS ALL YOU N

X SPOTS THE MARK's illustrated wedding invitation for a couple who met at a writing conference tells the story of their fairytale romance.

DETAILS

RESERVATIONS HAVE BEEN
MADE FOR WEDDING GUESTS AT
THE HOLLIS INN, 224 HOLLIS LANE
LAKELAND, FLORIDA.
PLEASE BOOK YOUR RESERVATION
NO LATER THAN MAY 15.
P | 223.265.6617
E | INFO@HOLLISGARDEN.COM

FOR FURTHER INFORMATION
PLEASE VISIT OUR WEDDING WEBSITE:
WWW.COLETTEANDHENRY.COM

COLETT
&
HENRY

HAVE CHOSEN THE FIRST DAY
OF THEIR NEW LIFE TOGETHER
AS SATURDAY, THE EIGHTEENTH OF JUNE
TWO THOUSAND SIXTEEN

YOU ARE INVITED TO SHARE IN THEIR JOY
AS THEY EXCHANGE MARRIAGE VOWS
AT FIVE O'CLOCK IN THE EVENING
HOLLIS GARDEN IN LAKELAND, FLORIDA

RECEPTION TO FOLLOW

RSVP

BY MAY FIRST

M_____

___ ACCEPTS WITH PLEASURE   ___ DECLINES WITH REGRET

Nº. ATTENDING ___

Floral Pleasures

After coming across this vintage floral etching, RACHEL MARVIN has built a whole invitation suite around it. The result is an elegant and modern design, which juxtaposes the delicate artwork with the rather masculine font.

Super Pop Modern

The **RUBAN COLLECTIF**'s Modernika
collection is a wild assortment of styles—
a fun way to announce a wedding
celebration with ephemera that embraces an
eclectic mix of colors, patterns,
and graphic design.

RSVP AVANT LE 15 FÉVRIER

TIMBRE

NOM: _____

○ Non, avec regretst   ○ Oui, avec plaisir !

○ Cocktail   ○ Dîner

Adultes: ___   Enfants: ___

DÎNER

AMANDINE
&
ALEXANDRE

VOUS ACCUEILLERONS
POUR UN DÎNER QUI SERA SERVI
AU CHÂTEAU PARADIS À PARTIR DE 20H .

Festive Feathers

SARAH THORNE's striking invitation to a fashion event in California features a die-cut envelope that unfolds to feathery perfection.

Designed around its seasonal autumn/winter English woodland theme, Sarah Thorne's invitation to Mulberry's party at the Coachella Valley Music and Arts Festival in California arrives in three pieces: an outer black envelope sealed with an over-sized sticker, an unfolding inner black layer of die-cut feathers, and a foiled board with event information in a gold that rivals the Californian sun. Typographer Craig Ward created the custom feather type, which is printed on G . F Smith Ebony Colorplan paper. ❮

Salon Shows
Sunday
20 February
10.15am
& 11.30am

Claridges
The Ballroom
Brook Street
Mayfair W1

RSVP
Cat Wickins
catw@mulberry.com
+44 7595 653 440
+44 207 491 4323

MULBERRY

Fortune Teller

An interactive invitation to Mulberry's
Autumn/Winter 2011 show, designed by SARAH THORNE,
showcases a pattern from the collection.

Presented in a folded fortune-teller format, Mulberry's Autumn/Winter 2011 show invitation by Sarah Thorne uses black uncoated paper that is screen printed in white with a busy hedgerow print. Gold foil highlights and an elegant feather typeface created by Craig Ward complete the look. Derived from the catwalk collection itself, the illustration is extended with additional hedgerow elements, including blackberries, birds, hedgehogs, and tangled leaves. Delivered to recipients in a rigid black box with a screen printed lid, the invitation unfolds to dramatically reveal the venue, date, and time. ❮

181

Unforgettable

SARAH THORNE's striking 3D invitation
to a fashion event guarantees that even the busiest
of invitees won't forget to attend.

When sending out invitations to busy journalists and PR people, it is imperative that the invite doesn't get lost in the shuffle. Designer Sarah Thorne's ingenious solution for Topshop and Vogue's catwalk event takes the form of a pop-up invitation. Arriving flat, it then assembles into a cube when removed from its envelope. Her bold use of typography, printed in a mix of black on white and white on black, ensures that the invitation eye-catchingly reminds each recipient of the big event. Both the time and date and the venue are featured across the mono-printed panels while coated stock with gloss UV varnish covers the black areas. ❮

SARAH THORNE's die-cut invitation to a Vogue Italia event at London's
Victoria & Albert Museum brings together a variety of materials and finishing
techniques to honor the fashion icon Anna Piaggi.

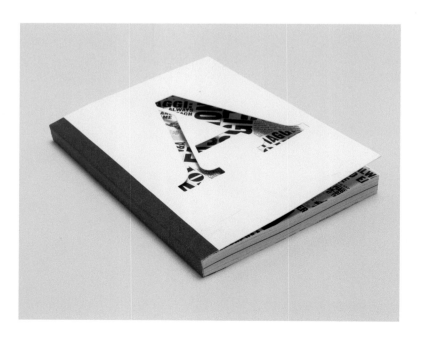

Fashion Week undoubtedly is a time when those involved are getting countless invitations. SARAH THORNE designed this inflatable rubber ring invite for a seaside themed Mulberry show that made sure the brand's event wouldn't get lost in the shuffle.

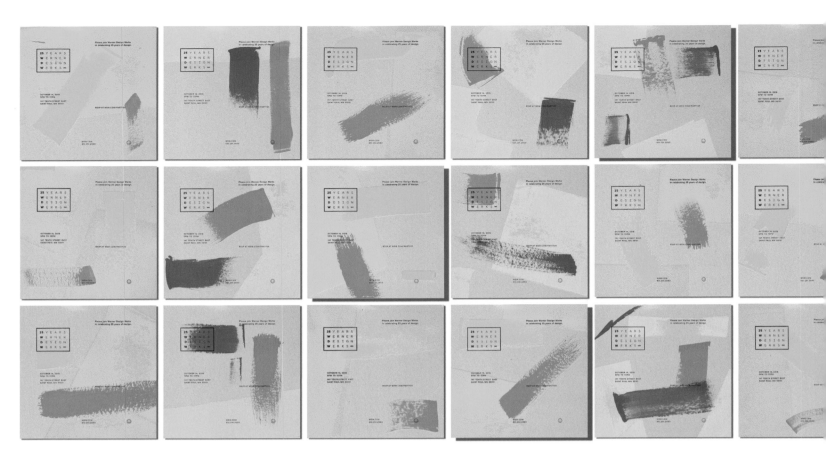

Work of Art

WERNER DESIGN WERKS's custom silver anniversary invitations gift guests with a piece of art.

When St. Paul-based Werner Design Werks celebrated its 25th anniversary in 2016, the three-person design studio did what 25 year olds do best: they threw a party. Looking for a way to make each invitation unique, the designers opted for an approach that combines printing and painting. To do this, they hand-painted several hundred pieces of 8 × 8 chipboard, then letterpressed the painted boards with black gloss foil. This easy, innovative method turned the invitations into individual pieces of art for every recipient. ‹

Flora and Fauna

TOKY's invitation for an environmental gala uses nature-driven illustrations to highlight its mission.

The Rainforest Alliance's annual gala is not just a party, but also an important fundraiser that helps sustain the organization throughout the coming year. For its 2015 event, the Alliance hired Toky to create a suite of event materials that would clearly communicate the organization's mission to conserve biodiversity. To do this, the designers used illustrations of flora and fauna intertwined with the typography, symbolizing the fact that every decision made by a consumer is bound with sustainability. The frog's-eye-view illustration, which appears across all of the collateral, echoes the organization's iconic frog logo. ❮

FROM THE DANCE FLOOR

TO THE

F
O
R
E
S
T

FLOOR

The Rainforest Alliance
Co-Chairs Costa Rica Tourism Board and Mattel, Inc.
invite you to the

RAINFOREST ALLIANCE GALA

WEDNESDAY, MAY 13, 2015

AMERICAN MUSEUM OF NATURAL HISTORY
Central Park West at 79th Street — Main Entrance
NEW YORK CITY

6:00 P.M. Cocktails & Silent Auction Opens
7:30 P.M. Dinner, Awards Ceremony & Entertainment

Formal Attire

For more information and reservations please visit
WWW.RAINFOREST-ALLIANCE.ORG/GALA

Domtar   TRAVELER   essential COSTA RICA

HONORING

LIFETIME ACHIEVEMENT AWARD
Marina Silva, Former Minister of Environment of Brazil

SUSTAINABLE STANDARD-SETTERS
Avery Dennison
Bettys & Taylors of Harrogate
Breyers
CMPC Forestal Mininco
Fibria

CELEBRATING THE ACHIEVEMENTS OF LEADERS, INNOVATORS, & CONSERVATIONISTS, WORKING TO PROTECT LAND & SUPPORT SUSTAINABLE LIVELIHOODS AROUND THE WORLD.

The Rainforest Alliance would like to express its appreciation to the following for their support of this event:

GREEN BENEFACTORS
Domtar
National Geographic Traveler

PREMIER BENEFACTORS
Avery Dennison
Luigi Lavazza S.p.A.

PLATINUM BENEFACTORS
Costa Rica Tourism Board
Fibria
Elysabeth Kleinhans
Nestlé Nespresso S.A.
Unilever

GOLD BENEFACTORS
Anonymous
AMResorts
Chiquita Brands International
Columbia Forest Products
Wendy Gordon & Larry Rockefeller
Lear Family Foundation
Lawrence & Victoria Lunt
Mattel, Inc.
Lise Strickler & Mark Gallogly

O'Melveny & Myers LLP
Staples, Inc.
YFY, Inc.

BRONZE BENEFACTORS
Bettys & Taylors of Harrogate
The Durst Organization
ENVIRON International Corporation
Goldman, Sachs & Co.
The JM Smucker Company
Laura & David Ross
Eric Rothenberg & Catherine Ludden
Annemieke Wijn

SILVER BENEFACTORS
Allegro Coffee Company
The Central National-
Gottesman Foundation
Citi
Clearwater Paper Corporation
CMPC Forestal Mininco
Talia & Seth Cohen
Roger & Sandy Deromedi
Marilú Hernández & Luis Bosoms
Maggie Lear & Daniel R. Katz
Munksjö Oyj

PATRONS
Daniel Cohen & Leah Keith
Jeffrey Kaufman
Kate Lear & Jon LaPook
Proyecto Mayakoba
Peter M. Schulte
Kerri & Drew Smith
USI Insurance Services, LLC
Alan & Karin Wilzig

BOARD OF DIRECTORS
Daniel R. Katz, Chair
Roger Deromedi, Vice Chair
Wendy Gordon, Vice Chair
Labeeb M. Abboud
Tasso Azevedo
Marilú Hernández de Bosoms
Gisele Bündchen
Seth Cohen
Sonila Cook
Daniel Couvreur
Lawrence Lunt
Count Amaury de Poret
David S. Ross
Eric Rothenberg
William Sarni
Peter M. Schulte
Kerri A. Smith
Annemieke Wijn

Tensie Whelan, President

Rainforest Alliance

233 Broadway, 28th floor · New York, NY 10279

DESIGNED BY TOKY.COM

FSC MIX Paper from responsible sources FSC® C020623

HONORING SUSTAINABLE
STANDARD-SETTERS

Avery Dennison
Bettys & Taylors of Harrogate
Breyers
Fibria
Forestal Mininco S.A.

For more information and reservations please visit
WWW.RAINFOREST-ALLIANCE.ORG/GALA

Domtar   TRAVELER

The Rainforest Alliance and Co-Chair Mattel, Inc. invite you to the

RAINFOREST ALLIANCE GALA

MAY 13, 2015
AMERICAN MUSEUM OF NATURAL HISTORY
NEW YORK CITY

CELEBRATE WITH US
for a few short hours
AND MAKE A LIFETIME OF DIFFERENCE.

Rainforest

Rainforest
Alliance

233 Broadway, 28th Floor
New York, NY 10279

T 212.677.1900 **F** 212.677.2187
www.rainforest-alliance.org

FROM THE DANCE FLOOR

TO THE

FOREST

FLOOR

RSVP

The Rainforest Alliance
Co-Chairs Costa Rica Tourism Board and Mattel, Inc.
invite you to the
RAINFOREST ALLIANCE GALA

WEDNESDAY, MAY 13, 2015

AMERICAN MUSEUM OF NATURAL HISTORY
Central Park West at 79th Street — Main Entrance
NEW YORK CITY

6:00 P.M. *Cocktails & Silent Auction Opens*
7:30 P.M. *Dinner, Awards Ceremony & Entertainment*

Formal Attire

For more information and reservations please visit
WWW.RAINFOREST-ALLIANCE.ORG/GALA

Domtar   **TRAVELER**   *essential* COSTA RICA

A NIGHT OF REVELRY

MAY 13, 2015

Rainforest Alliance

SAVE THE date

"and we created you in pairs"

Elegantly Whimsical

Botanical illustrations for an Indonesian wedding invitation by **HARI BAHAGIA** capture a vintage vibe with a modern twist for this tropically inspired celebration.

THANK YOU

SURYA · POPPIE

CINNAMON

LEMONGRASS

COCONUT

Vintage Blooms

Designer **VIVEK VENKATRAMAN** created save the date cards with a bloom of botanicals taken from a beautifully drawn book of the 1990s that features Arizona's desert flowers.

SAVE THE DATE

Designer **VIVEK VENKATRAMAN** created save the date cards with a bloom of botanicals taken from a beautifully drawn book of the 1990s that features Arizona's desert flowers.

Locks
and Keys

To celebrate the store opening of the luxury wedding store BHLDN in Beverly Hills, MEAGHAN MURRAY designed these exquisite invitations in form of golden keys, that are reminiscent of those one receives at the reception of a luxurious hotel.

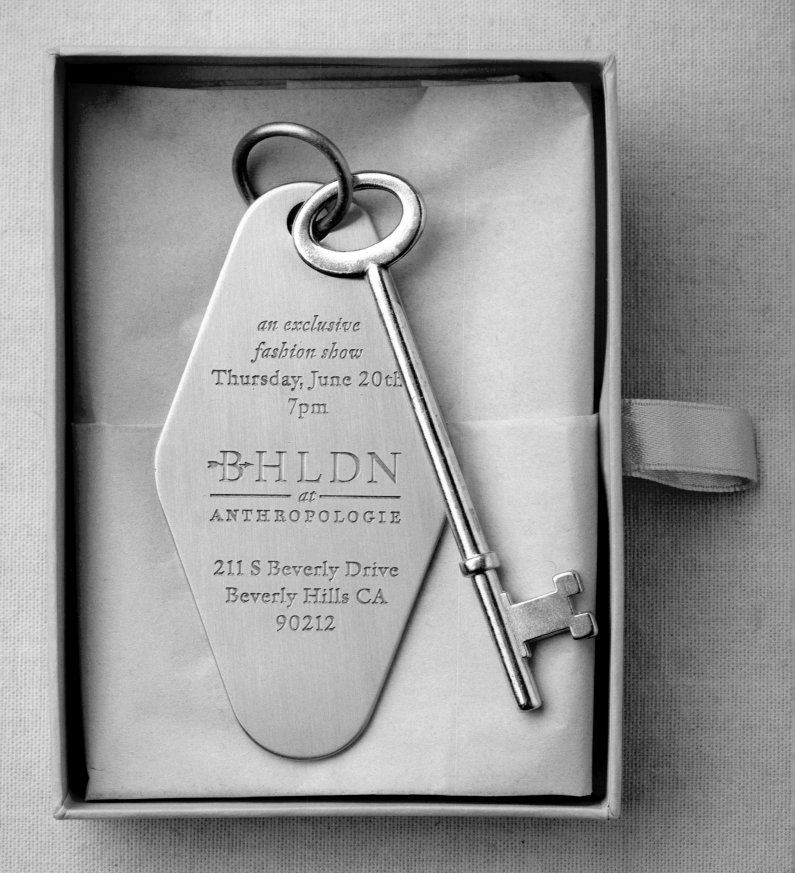

*an exclusive
fashion show*
Thursday, June 20th
7pm

BHLDN
at
ANTHROPOLOGIE

211 S Beverly Drive
Beverly Hills CA
90212

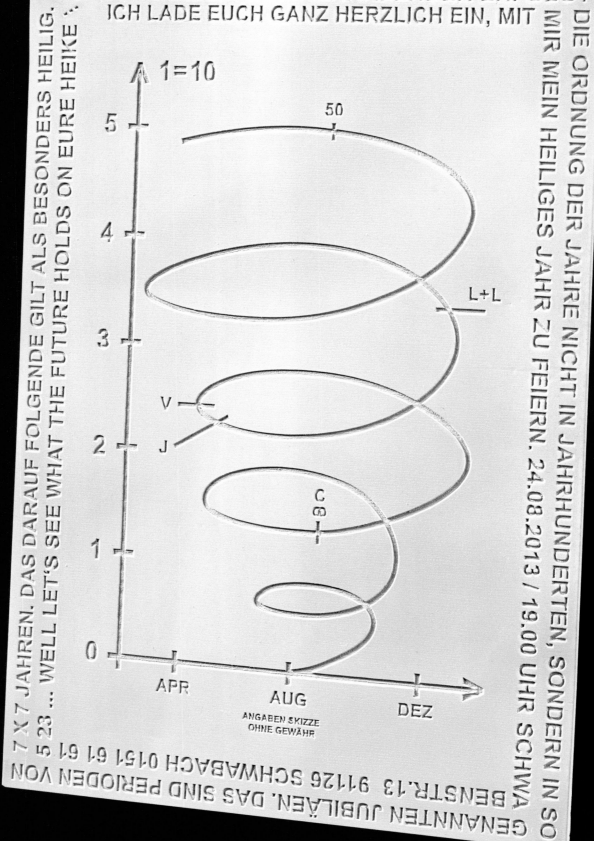

Milestone Achievement

A porcelain invitation by **VERENA HENNIG** uses this precious material to symbolize a special anniversary.

This award-winning 50th anniversary invitation by Verena Hennig takes a different approach to the typical designs used for such an occasion. Instead of working with paper, the designer used porcelain to highlight the reason for the celebration; its qualities as a precious, traditional, and timeless material perfectly symbolize the importance of a 50-year milestone. Details were die cut into the porcelain, which was then fired in a conventional ceramic furnace and produced as a limited edition of 50—what else? ❮

STUART AND GILLIAN MACEY

INVITE YOU TO CELEBRATE

THE MARRIAGE OF THEIR DAUGHTER

Victoria
Sa

AT FOUR

PAL

R.S.V.P.

PLEASE RSVP ONLINE BY MARCH 2016

VICTORIAANDSASHA.COM

IT WOULD M
IF YOU'D
AT THE KO

YOU

Bedou

call (760) 86-

Mr.

Sa

9

Desert Vibes

Wedding invitations by VICTORIA MACEY strike the perfect stylistic balance for a Palm Springs wedding.

The biggest challenge for Victoria Macey when designing her own wedding invitations was to avoid a common wedding industry trend by instead making them as gender neutral as possible. Her goal was a design that felt authentic to her and her husband's personal styles, while also evoking a rustic, desert vibe to reflect the Palm Springs venue. She achieved the perfect balance between the two with a clean san serif type mixed with bold, full-bleed hand-lettering. The minimal color palette brings sophistication and gender neutrality to the final piece, while cacti illustrations cue the desert vibe and add a hand-crafted touch. ‹

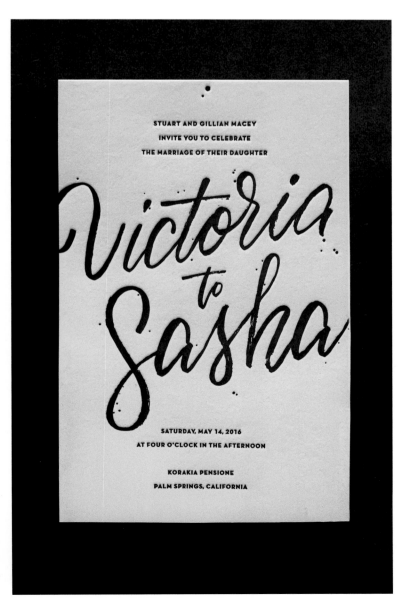

STUART AND GILLIAN MACEY
INVITE YOU TO CELEBRATE
THE MARRIAGE OF THEIR DAUGHTER

Victoria to Sasha

SATURDAY, MAY 14, 2016
AT FOUR O'CLOCK IN THE AFTERNOON

KORAKIA PENSIONE
PALM SPRINGS, CALIFORNIA

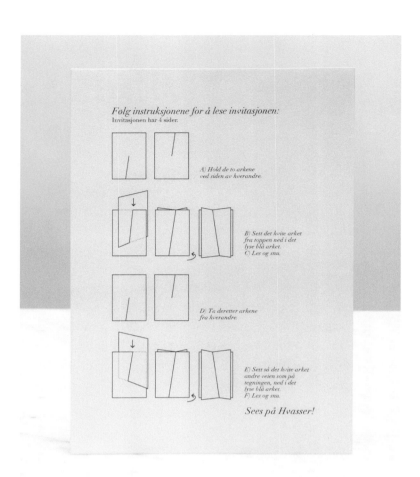

Følg instruksjonene for å lese invitasjonen:
Invitasjonen har 4 sider.

A) Hold de to arkene
ved siden av hverandre.

B) Sett det hvite arket
fra toppen ned i det
lyse blå arket.
C) Les og snu.

D) Ta deretter arkene
fra hverandre.

E) Sett så det hvite arket
andre veien som på
tegningen, ned i det
lyse blå arket.
F) Les og snu.

Sees på Hvasser!

It Takes Two

A clever wedding invitation by OLSSØN BARBIERI cannot be read without assembling two parts into one.

Designers Henrik Olssøn and Erika Barbieri of Olssøn Barbieri created a wedding invitation with an interesting twist for two good friends. Their concept uses two cards, each containing different details about the day, that must be put together in order to be legible. To achieve this, the cards use a transversal cut that allows invitees to read the content only when the two are intersected. By unlocking and reconnecting the cards in opposite directions, one can read the other two sides for a total of four pages. An instruction sheet accompanied the invitation, which was letterpressed on G . F Smith Colorplan paper, using an ivory white color with a Didot font for the bride, and a sky blue color with a Grotesque font for the groom. ❮

KAR RE GLEDE ITERE
+
SON ING AV SONDRES LUP
SA DAG GUST 2013.

Joan & Reidar

Marit & Stein   OG

Har den sto IN
av å inv
til feir DRE
Karin og
Bryl =
lør NT
den 24. Au

KAR IN
+
SON DRE
=
SA NT

Marit & Stein   OG   Joan & Reidar

Har den sto RE GLEDE
av å inv ITERE
til feir ING AV
Karin og SONDRES
Bryl LUP
lør DAG
den 24. Au GUST 2013.

Happiest Day

A wedding invitation by **MIRAE KIM** uses Korean fonts to create a unique look.

Based on a gridded design, Mirae Kim's wedding invitation for a Korean couple uses various round Korean fonts to create a fresh look, and a line drawing to capture the couple's likeness. The boldly colored vintage illustrations depict the couple's sense of humor and add an individual note to each of the suites' variations. Complementary colors and simple, yet playful imagery intensify the warm feel of the invites and definitely make a delightful keepsake for the wedding's guests. ‹

Being playful within a strict grid is not a contradiction in Mirae Kim's designs.

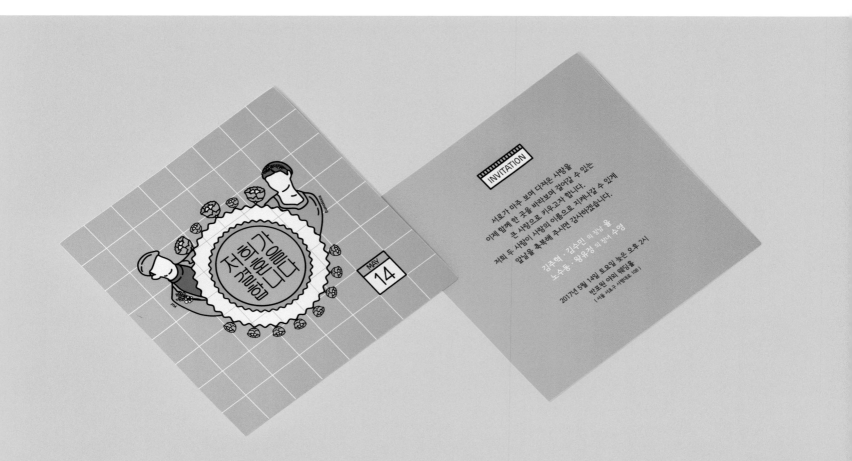

A gente cuida, a gente olha,

A gente deixa o sol bater pra crescer, pra crescer

A rosa do amor tem sempre que crescer

A rosa do amor não vai despetalar

Treasure Trove

Designer **ISABELLA TELES** creates
an invitation in a box that delights guests as
they unpack its contents.

The concepts surrounding Bernardo and Isabella's wedding invitation were delicacy, flowers, garden, nature, treasure, and harmony. With these ideas in mind, designer Isabella Teles created the couple's logo, save the date card, invitation, and other materials for the ceremony. The invitation arrived inside a box that also contained a photo in a vintage frame, a small leaflet with information and tips, poems, and intricate bird illustrations. Printed on both Design Pale Cream and Couché paper, Teles used hot foil stamping on the logo to represent the value of the deeply meaningful day. ❮

The Bond of Love

Two touching hands are a strong symbol of love and genuine human connection. Resulting from a spontaneous idea, Seth Conley of **THE BEAUTIFUL FAILURE**, photographer Shaun Mendiola, and hand-lettering artist Steve Luker created this one-of-a-kind wedding invite.

ytales

JON MARCHIONE's style is reminiscent of those illustrations we're encounter in children's books. Combining this with custom hand-lett has recreated that magic in a botanical illustration for a wedding

Seeking for an alternative to boring invitation
templates, James and Alexa Hirschfeld created Paperless Post and
disrupted the stationery business.

Paperless Post

New York City [USA]

A good invitation needs to break the rules a bit. This has been Paperless Post's guiding philosophy since founder James Hirschfeld was a college student approaching his 21st birthday. With an elaborate birthday party planned, he found that there were no quality options for an online invitation. Luckily, the dilemma sparked an innovative idea, and together with his sister, Alexa, Hirschfeld launched Paperless Post two years later, creating a much-needed online platform for beautifully designed communications.

Sending online invitations solves many of the common headaches that come with event-planning territory; it is easy to see who has received and opened their invitation, and RSVPs become infinitely easier to manage and receive. But certain elements of traditional paper invitations get lost in the digital format, including the tactile qualities of paper and the experience of opening a hand-addressed envelope that's arrived in the mail. Finding a

Paperless Post often partners up with renowned illustrators and designers to create capsule stationery collections. Their collaboration with Rifle Paper Co. resulted in a selection of whimsical floral designs for every occasion.

PLEASE JOIN BESSIE *and* LES GLASS

for ROSÉ *on* THE ROOF

SATURDAY, JUNE 12TH | *at* 2PM | 101 CENTRAL PARK WEST

TOGETHER WITH THEIR FAMILIES

RENÉE
SAINT-MÉRAN
&
GÉRARD
VILLEFORT

REQUEST YOUR PRESENCE
AT THE CEREMONY AND CELEBRATION
OF THEIR MARRIAGE
SUNDAY, THE FIFTH OF DECEMBER
EIGHTEEN HUNDRED AND FORTY FIVE
AT ELEVEN IN THE MORNING
CHÂTEAU D'IF, MARSEILLE

RECEPTION TO FOLLOW

DIRECTIONS
CHÂTEAU D'IF
1, QUAI DE LA FRATER
BOAT DEPARTURES FROM THE QUAI DE
(OLD PORT) NEAR CANNEBIÈRE

ACCOMMODATI
LE P
+
FOR YOUR CONVEN
ROOMS. PLEASE
WEDDING W

SAVE THE DATE

JUNE 10, 1953 | NEW YORK

STELLA & AUGUST

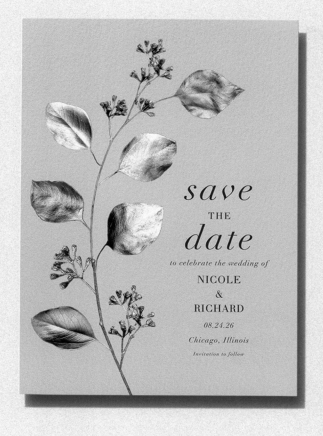

save
THE
date
to celebrate the wedding of
NICOLE
&
RICHARD
08.24.26
Chicago, Illinois
Invitation to follow

DIRECTIONS

PROMONTORY POINT
BURNHAM PARK
5491 SOUTH LAKE SHORE DRIVE

FROM I-90, TRAVEL EAST ON EAST 67TH STREET.
TAKE A LEFT ONTO SOUTH JEFFERY AVENUE.
STAY ON SOUTH JEFFERY AVENUE
AS IT BECOMES SOUTH LAKE SHORE DRIVE.

ACCOMMODATIONS

HYDE PARK ARMS HOTEL
5316 SOUTH HARPER AVENUE

F
WE HAVE
PLEASE MEN
WHEN

PLEASE REPLY BY

JUNE FOURTEENTH
M _____

____ JOYFULLY ACCEPT
____ REGRETFULLY DECLINE

PLEASE SELECT AN ENTRÉE

_ FILET MIGNON _ WILD-CAUGHT SALMON _ PASTA PRIMAVERA

Y BY

FULLY DECLINE

LINA ZIZMO IS THROWING A

BABY SHOWER

IN HONOR OF TESSIE STEPHANIDES

SATURDAY, AUGUST 17TH AT 2PM

524 MIDDLESEX BOULEVARD

GROSSE POINTE

way to mirror the qualities of paper in an online format led the team to offer options such as deckled edges and calligraphy. Perhaps more importantly, they were able to digitally recreate the ritual of opening an envelope to reveal the card inside.

In the years since Paperless Post's founding, there has been a definite shift back to printed invitations, as consumers crave the tactile experience of holding an object in their hands—or even hanging it on the wall as a decorative piece. In keeping up with the market and acknowledging that their users have shifting needs, Paperless Press decided to venture into the world of printed invitations. Now each design they offer is available in either digital or printed format.

Whether digital or printed, long gone are the days of traditional invitation etiquette, which valued conformity over expression of personal aesthetics. Invitations generally looked alike due to stock wording, fonts, and paper. Now it is easy to personalize any event, something Paperless Post knows all about. Partnering with a group of curated illustrators and designers, they offer users a wide range of styles to brand their event. Working with experienced creatives like Confetti System and Cabana Magazine also means offering trendsetting designs. Florals can be transformed into something unlike what has been

PLEASE JOIN HAZEL & FIVER FOR AN

EASTER EGG HUNT & PICNIC LUNCH

SUNDAY, APRIL 20TH AT NOON
SANDLEFORD PARK

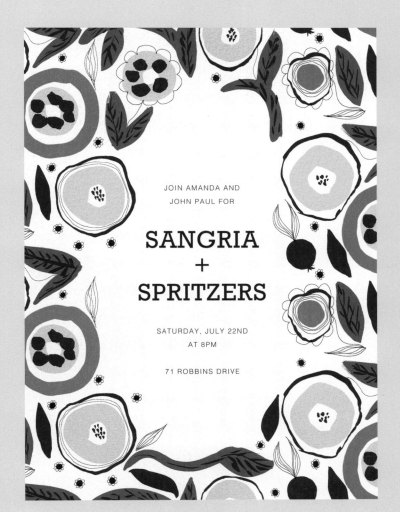

JOIN AMANDA AND
JOHN PAUL FOR

SANGRIA + SPRITZERS

SATURDAY, JULY 22ND
AT 8PM

71 ROBBINS DRIVE

Another collaboration that proved to be a full success was the one with the Finnish design house Marimekko. Reinterpreting some of their legendary patterns, the brand designed quirky and colorful templates for thank-you notes, party invitations, and personalized stationery.

seen before. These designers are able to take something as timeless as gold foil and give it a new look—take, for instance, the current trend of pairing its luxurious aesthetic with humorous and unexpected text.

For someone as well-versed in the culture of invitation design as Hirschfeld, it is impossible not to ask him about the most memorable invitation that has found its way into his hands. The answer? A hand-painted wedding invitation by the master of modern calligraphy, Bernard Maisner—which, incidentally, you can now find in a digital version on Paperless Post. ‹

DID YOU SAY "COCK'S TAIL" OR "COCKTAIL"?

EITHER WAY,
WE NEED A DRINK.

LET'S CATCH UP OVER
COCKTAILS & CHARCUTERIE
WEDNESDAY JUNE ELEVENTH
AT SEVEN O'CLOCK IN THE EVENING
BAR BOULUD | 1900 BROADWAY | NEW YORK

RSVP

YES, THERE WILL BE AN OPEN BAR

COME CELEBRATE OUR TRUE LOVE AND EVERLASTING COMMITMENT.

Saturday, October 15th
at seven in the evening

123 Fake Street
New York City

RSVP | no gifts please

Martha and George invite you for

COCKTAILS

and

CONVERSATION

April 14th at 9pm

15 Woolf Street • New Carthage

RSVP

join us

"A good invitation needs to break the rules a little bit."

JAMES HIRSCHFELD

henry
WILCOX

request your presence
at the ceremony
& celebration
of their marriage
saturday, may thirteenth
nineteen hundred & ten
at six thirty in the evening
howards end
hertfordshire

reception to follow

their families

tt
ey

ael
bell

on

TOGETHER WITH THEIR FAMILIES

LUCY
HONEYCHURCH

AND

GEORGE
EMERSON

REQUEST YOUR PRESENCE
AT THE CEREMONY AND CELEBRATION
OF THEIR MARRIAGE

SATURDAY, DECEMBER FIRST
NINETEEN EIGHTY FIVE
AT FIVE IN THE EVENING
PENSIONE BERLOTINI
FLORENCE
RECEPTION TO FOLLOW

STELLA & AUGUST
JUNE 10, 1953

HAMILTON

REQUEST YOUR PRESENCE
AT THE CEREMONY AND CELEBRATION
OF THEIR MARRIAGE
SATURDAY, AUGUST TWELFTH
NINETEEN HUNDRED AND SIXTY FIVE
AT THREE IN THE AFTERNOON
SUNSET HOTEL | NEGARA, BALI

RECEPTION TO FOLLOW

B R E
A N
M I C H
7 . 2 1 .

MADRID | INVITATION TO FOLLOW

SAVE THE DATE

JANE
AND
EDWARD

AUGUST 21, 1847 | HATHERSAGE, DERBYSHIRE
INVITATION TO FOLLOW

IT'S JANE'S BIG DAY!
JOIN US AS WE THROW HER
A VERY SPECIAL
10TH BIRTHDAY PARTY
FRIDAY, AUGUST 28TH AT 4PM
15 CHERRY TREE LANE
LONDON

CELEBRATE DAVID'S
9TH BIRTHDAY
WITH AN AFTERNOON
OF VIDEO GAMES

SATURDAY, MAY 7TH AT 3:30PM
4560 EAST OLIVE STREET | SEATTLE

BENJAMIN'S
18TH BIRTHDAY

SATURDAY, JUNE 2, 3 PM

THE POOL DECK AT THE TAFT HOTEL
3400 WILSHIRE BOULEVARD, LOS ANGELES

Each design is available in a digital or printed format.

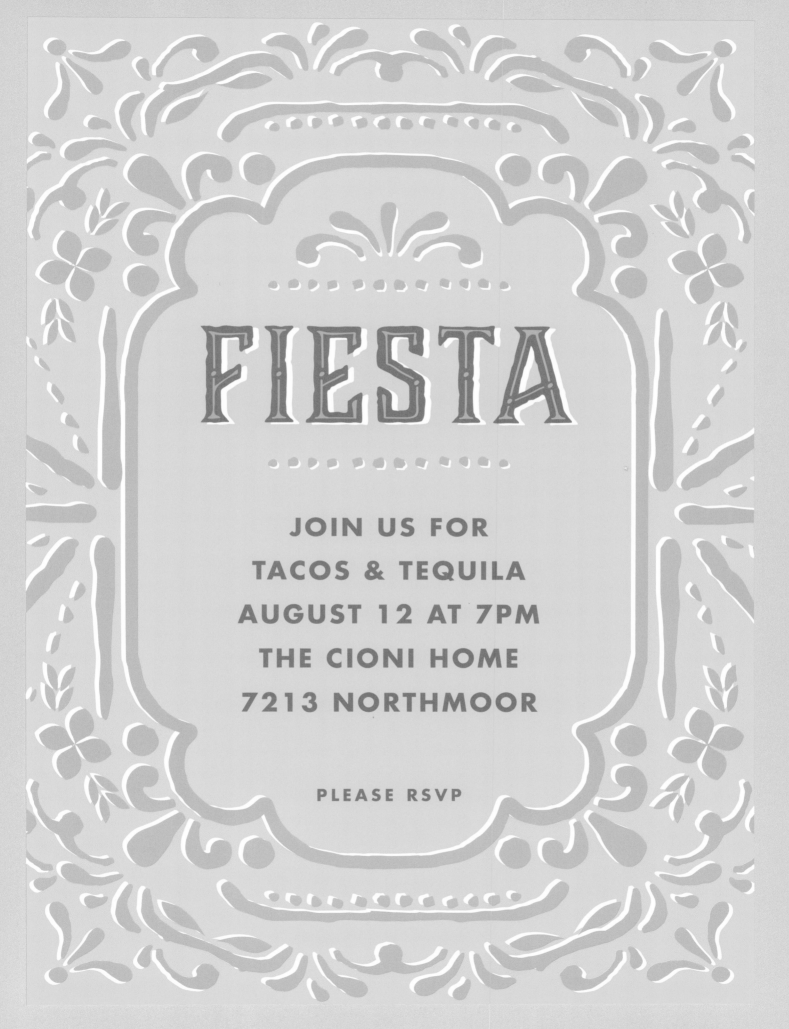

FIESTA

JOIN US FOR
TACOS & TEQUILA
AUGUST 12 AT 7PM
THE CIONI HOME
7213 NORTHMOOR

PLEASE RSVP

Cut It Out

CUTTURE's laser-cut pop-up invitations
deliver a stand-out design for a holiday party
at London's iconic Royal Opera House.

A holiday event hosted by McKinsey & Company at London's
Royal Opera House dictated a stand-out invitation that would
guarantee a great attendance rate. The company commissioned
Cutture to create the festive invite, which included a nod to
the infamous architecture of the venue, as well as a cheerful
holiday feel and winter aesthetic. The final piece used a pop-up
format that could accompany the intricate laser-cut details of
the building, and also incorporated the company's corporate
colors and typography. ❮

RSVP

Please reply to confirm your attendance to either

HELEN GILKES
020 7961 6766
HELEN_GILKES@EXTERNAL.MCKINSEY.COM

OR

SARAH BEAN
020 7961 5502
SARAH_BEAN@MCKINSEY.COM

IF YOU HAVE ANY DIETARY REQUIREMENTS
PLEASE DON'T HESITATE
TO CONTACT US.

Heart to Type

JILL DE HAAN's love for hand-lettering translates perfectly into an elegant and playful take on a save the date card and a baptism invitation, both reminiscent of vintage postcards.

Save the Date for the joyful union of Ben & Montana, June 28th, 2014, Rock Creek, MT, Invitation to Follow

Folklore Tales

The Bucharest-based illustrator MADALINA ANDRONIC draws inspiration for her illustrated invitations from traditional Romanian fairy tales and folklore.

ANNA + JOHN

request the honor of your company
at the celebration of their union
Saturday, 10th of June 2017
at 12 o'clock in the afternoon

Arctic Club Hotel, 700 Third Avenue
Seattle, Washington

Dinner and dancing to follow

details

After the ceremony,
join us for an evening reception.
Cocktails and hors d'oeuvres at 5:00pm
Dinner will be served at 6:00pm
dancing and merriment to follow.

Transportation will be provided
to and from wedding ceremony
and reception.
Shuttles will depart from the hotel lobby
45 minutes prior to each event
and return every half-hour
beginning at 9 pm.

ANNA + JOHN

save the date
10.06.2017

EMMA THOMPSON

ANNA + JOH
10 June 20

Thank you for a wonderful d

RSVP

kindly reply until June 1st

__ can't wait

__ can't make it

send us this card in the mail at
8 Flower St., Seattle
or drop us a line at annaandjohn@us.com

12

menu

ENTREE
House Mixed Lettuces, Shallot and Thyme Vinaigrette,
Candied Pecans, Dried Cherries, Brie Cheese

MAIN
Nagano Pork Tenderloin with Grainy Mustard Demi-Glace,
Served with Roasted Garlic Fork Mash and Fresh Vegetables

DESSERT
Mascarpone Cheesecake with Lemon, Cherries,
Cocoa Nibs and Vanilla Bean Espuma

(P)op-Art Vanities

MALIKA FAVRE is an acclaimed illustrator renowned for her delicate
use of negative/positive space and color. If you happen to be one of her friends,
she might come up with an irresistibly stylish design for your invites.

Party Time

YONDER's birthday invitation
for a Cuban-themed fete comes with the
fixings for a good time.

A birthday party with an all-out Cuban theme to be held at the Starlight Social Club needed a big dose of Cuban flair. So the designers at Yonder ditched the simple paper invitation for a more spectacular one that arrived in an antique cigar box. The package comes complete with a mojito kit for a pre-party cocktail, and includes vibrant images that hint at each of the weekend's events—from Cuban cigars to old cars in a Havana sunset. When receiving such festive bounty, who wouldn't want to attend? ❮

Personal Touch

NATHAN YODER illustrates unique keepsake wedding invitations for his family.

It has become tradition for illustrator Nathan Yoder to illustrate and design the wedding invitations for his many siblings. For his little sister, he poured years of memories and friendship into the design, creating an original illustration with dip pen, which was ultimately printed using metallic inks. For his youngest brother Zach's wedding—the last to get married—he wanted to make the invitation extra special, choosing to draw a portrait of his brother and now sister-in-law Rachel in pen and ink. The final piece, influenced by ornate announcements of the 1930s and 1940s, is hand-lettered and printed as an offset lithograph. ❮

Linocut Story

Invitations to this Greek-Russian
wedding by IYA GAAS feature illustrations that
tell the story of a couple's heritage.

When Iya Gaas set out to design wedding invitations for a
Greek-Russian wedding, it was the nationalities of the couple
that most inspired the designer's concept. Choosing the linocut
technique, the invite features a female matryoshka depicted in
the Russian ornamental style, while the male figure is drawn in
the national costume of Greece. A blue and red color palette
encompasses the national colors of both countries. This unique
piece gave guests a preview of the beautiful celebration they
had to look forward to, which honored two rich traditions. ‹

New Beginnings

Asia Forbes of **BOLDHOUSE CREATIVE** has created this wedding suite for a couple that cherishes nature and outdoor living. The main invitation, featuring a fern, is accompanied by a custom hand-lettered typeface influenced by art deco typography.

RUBY & DAN
invite you to join them
to celebrate their marriage
25th november 2017
at two o'clock

•

BROCKHOLES WOOD
reception to follow

Woodland

Elegant yet playful, the papercut inspired wedding stationery collection by EMMA JO creates a little woodland
world by using simple organic shapes and inserting hidden creatures.

Flamingo Fabulous

Florida-inspired invitations by **CECI NEW YORK** for a destination wedding showcase the area's unmistakable aesthetic. Taking center stage is an original illustration by Ceci Johnson that features a palm tree and flamingo backdrop with a gold foil-stamped crest on top.

241

1497 THOMAS DR.
NAPA, CA 94558
L & J

TOGETHER WITH THEIR FAMILIES

LEVI RAY & JENNIFER MARIE

INVITE YOU TO JOIN THEM IN THE
CELEBRATION OF THEIR UNION
FRIDAY MARCH 20, 2015 AT 3:30 IN THE AFTERNOON
1497 THOMAS DRIVE NAPA, CALIFORNIA

DINNER & MERRIMENT TO FOLLOW

RSVP

WILL ATTEND _____
WITH REGRETS _____

Please RSVP by Feb 22

MARCH 20

LEVI
&
JEN

SAVE THE

Highly Symbolic

These invites by SHIPWRIGHT & CO. announce
an unconventional backyard wedding.

Each piece of Jen and Levi's invitation has an alchemy-inspired design, including the clasped hands featured on the ring, which were also used on the save the date cards. Because the couple also included elements of handfasting in their ceremony, they wanted Shipwright & Co. to reflect its symbolism in the invitation. The couple chose to have a small ceremony in their backyard, so they also sent out announcements to friends and family who weren't able to attend. ❮

Fashion Show

ROANDCO's design for a
fashion brand's debut collection embodies
its personality and style.

The high-end women's luxury brand Honor translates the nostalgia of an old-world atelier into something sophisticated, wearable, and modern. Having already designed the company's branding, RoAndCo returned to art direct the presentation and campaign shoot for its debut collection in 2011. To build anticipation for the show, VIPs received boxes filled with macaroons as well as an invitation lined with the signature Spring/Summer 2011 floral pattern. For the runway show, RoAndCo designed the set as a series of vignettes including a bedroom, a party, and a golf game, where the models could embody different elements of the Honor woman. ❮

CELEBRATING
175
YEARS OF
FLAVOUR

Knorr®

Join us for a
FREE
LUNCH
on 18th October

Green Thumb

JONES KNOWLES RITCHIE exchanges
paper for herbs in this unconventional take
on a luncheon invitation.

It is not often that a company can celebrate 175 years in business, but Knorr had just such an occasion in 2013. To mark the milestone, they commissioned Jones Knowles Ritchie to design an invitation for the celebratory lunch. To embody the nature of such an event, as well as reflect the heart of the Knorr brand—a love of flavor—the designers thought beyond a piece of paper. They found an innovative solution in a pot of herbs, sending 800 guests basil and rosemary with the details of the event (and a Knorr recipe) written on the pot wrappers and tags. ❮

SAVANNAH TAYLOR has designed these botanical save the dates for a summer wedding in the southwest of France.

RÉSERVEZ LA DATE

JOSEPH
AND
NATASHA

14TH-17TH JULY 2017
URVAL, FRANCE

FORMAL INVITATION TO FOLLOW

Field Feast

The annual Lowcountry Field Feast intends to bring awareness to the local farmers and independent businesses. STITCH DESIGN CO. came up with a design that provided all the relevant details and served as a delicious amuse-bouche for the event.

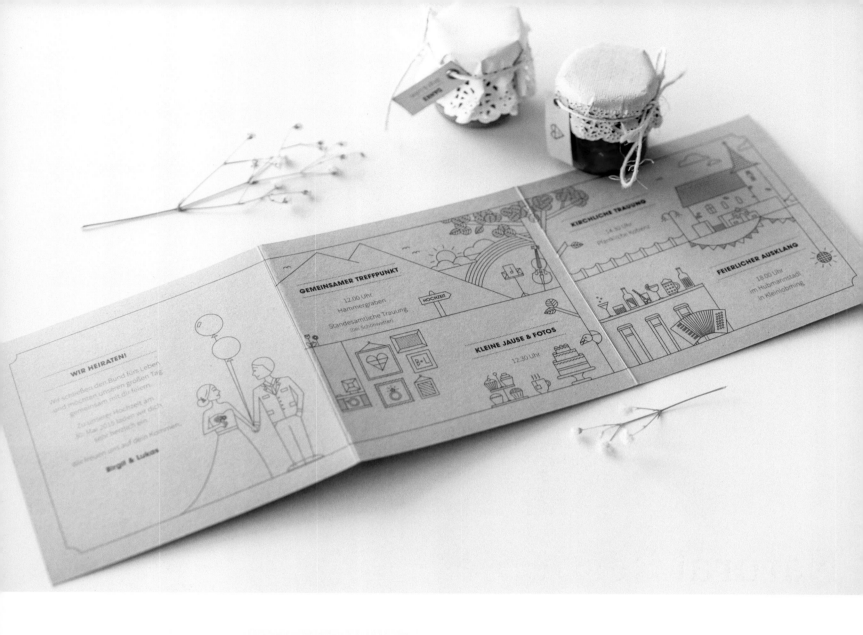

Austrian Rustic

A countryside wedding invitation by KATRIN KOHL mixes modern design with an organic sensibility.

Birgit and Lukas's wedding in the Austrian countryside called for an invitation that reflected their love of nature. Designer Katrin Kohl started by developing a logo that uses their initials to form a geometric heart—a design element that immediately catches the eye when spotted through the transparent envelope. The logo also makes an appearance on small jars of jam for the guests and on thank you notes. Once opened, the three-fold invitation uses vector illustrations alongside the text to illustrate fun details about the couple. Printed on eco-friendly Crush paper by Favini and colored with residues from organic materials like olives and kiwis, the invitations perfectly suit the spirit of this rustic backyard wedding. ❮

Natural Resources

Knowing that the wedding will take place in the shadows of a giant willow tree, YONDER came up with this concept that prominently features wild moss.

Designer Index A–M

Designer Index N–Z

YOU'RE INVITED!

Invitation Design
for Every Occasion

This book was conceived, edited, and designed by Gestalten.

Edited by Robert Klanten and Anja Kouznetsova

Text and Preface by Rebecca Silus

Project Management by Sina Kernstock

Design and Layout by Benjamin Wolbergs
Creative Direction of Design by Ludwig Wendt

Typefaces: ITC Cheltenham by Tony Stan;
Client Mono by O. Lindqvist, S. Wadsted (Foundry: gestaltenfonts.com)

Cover Design by Daniel Ioannou

Printed by Grafisches Centrum Cuno GmbH & Co. KG, Calbe
Made in Germany

Published by Gestalten, Berlin 2017
ISBN 978-3-89955-920-0

©Die Gestalten Verlag GmbH & Co. KG, Berlin 2017
All rights reserved. No part of this publication may be reproduced or transmitted
in any form or by any means, electronic or mechanical, including photocopy or any storage
and retrieval system, without permission in writing from the publisher.

Respect copyrights, encourage creativity!

For more information, and to order books, please visit www.gestalten.com.

Bibliographic information published by the Deutsche Nationalbibliothek.
The Deutsche Nationalbibliothek lists this publication in the Deutsche Nationalbiblio-
grafie; detailed bibliographic data are available online at http://dnb.d-nb.de.

None of the content in this book was published in exchange for payment by commercial parties or designers; Gestalten selected all included work based solely on its artistic merit.

This book was printed on paper certified according to the standards of the FSC®.